Learning in Embedded Systems

Learning in Embedded Systems

Leslie Pack Kaelbling

A Bradford Book
The MIT Press
Cambridge, Massachusetts
London, England

This book was set in Palatino by TechBooks and was printed and bound in the United States of America.

Kaelbling, Leslie Pack.
  Learning in embedded systems / Leslie Pack Kaelbling.
    p.   cm.
  "A Bradford book."
  Includes bibliographical references and index.
  ISBN 0-262-11174-8
  1. Embedded computer systems--Programming.   2. Computer algorithms.   I. Title.
QA76.6.K333   1993
006.3'1--dc20   92-24672
                                                         CIP

To the memory of my parents, who taught me I could do anything if I tried.

Contents

Chapter 7
A Generate-and-Test Algorithm   89

Chapter 8
Learning Action Maps with State   113

Acknowledgments

My first thanks go to Stan Rosenschein. He has been a colleague and mentor, providing me with lots of ideas, criticism and inspiration, and with two excellent environments for carrying out research. Thanks to John McCarthy for getting me interested in AI and to Nils Nilsson for making me go back to school before I forgot how. Rich Sutton helped me to ground my work in the context of existing literatures I had never heard of and suggested interesting extensions of my basic ideas. Jeff Kerr and Stanley Reifel have provided robots to play with and lots of help and good advice. David Chapman, Stan Rosenschein, Rich Sutton and Nils Nilsson provided insightful comments on drafts of the dissertation on which this book is based; they have helped the clarity of the exposition considerably. Many other colleagues at Stanford, CSLI, SRI and Teleos have helped in indirect but important ways. David Kaelbling has been kind and patient beyond measure through all this and the pygmies appreciate it.

This work was supported in part by the Air Force Office of Scientific Research under contract F49620-89-C-0055, in part by the System Development Foundation, and in part by Teleos Research IR&D.

Learning in Embedded Systems

Chapter 1
Introduction

An *embedded system* has an ongoing interaction with a dynamic external world. Embedded systems may be physically embodied or may be purely computational. Mobile robots, factory process controllers, and calendar-managing programs are examples of embedded systems. They are expected to run for extended periods of time, repeatedly processing new input data and generating output data. They are embedded in environments whose dynamics they can influence, but cannot completely control.

Every embedded system has perceptual faculties through which it can sense aspects of the state of its environment; it also has effectors that it can use to influence the state of the environment. The behavior of most embedded systems can be described by a mapping from percepts to effector outputs; the mapping may have internal state, allowing the effector outputs to, potentially, depend on the entire previous history of percepts. The system continually examines the state of the environment through perception, then executes the appropriate effector outputs as specified by the mapping.

The external environment is likely to be changing during the interval between the embedded system's examination of its percepts and its execution of outputs. Exactly how the environment changes will depend on, among other things, the length of the interval. In order for a system to make appropriate and reliable responses to environmental conditions, there must be a predictable bound on the length of this interval. We will refer to behaviors with a bounded response time as being *real time*.

In general, the perceptual abilities of the system will be insufficient to completely characterize the state of the external environment. This means that, in many cases, taking the same action in states of the external environment that appear to be the same will cause different results. Thus, even in deterministic environments, the data that the system gets may be inconsistent, or *noisy*.

1.1 Direct Programming

The traditional approach to building embedded systems has been to program them. Simple controllers are built using techniques of logical specification and of procedural programming, but, as the systems that we wish to build become more complex, the programming task becomes increasingly difficult.

Because embedded systems must operate in dynamic environments that are not entirely predictable, their behavior is typically highly conditional, making it difficult to describe in conventional procedural programming languages. A variety of new programming methodologies that attempt to simplify the problems of programming embedded systems have been developed within the artificial intelligence (AI) community [15, 30, 42]. Systems constructed using these techniques are often described as *reactive*, because their actions are typically thought of as reactions to recent perceptual information rather than as steps in a complex, preconceived plan.

The designer of an embedded system is given a specification of an environment or a class of environments in which the system must work and a specification of the task the system is to perform. The environment description may include the physical morphology and primitive sensorimotor capabilities of the system, or those may be left to vary as part of the design. The word "task" is used very broadly here: a task could be as simple as to keep moving without bumping into things or as complex as to research the geological make-up of an unexplored planet. Because we are interested in systems that have a long-term interaction with an environment, tasks will not be specifications of short-term achievement goals that terminate before the end of the system's "life."

Even with appropriate programming languages and task specifications, programming embedded agents is quite difficult.

It is theoretically possible, given complete and correct specifications of the task and the environment, to design a system that optimally carries out the task in the environment. However, this strict prerequisite is rarely, if ever, satisfied. Even when it *is* satisfied, the information is quite often given in a form that the human programmer is unable to exploit directly:

> I once spent a long time trying to program a mobile robot to use ultrasonic sensors to navigate down a hallway. I had a physical specification of the environment (it was the hallway I was sitting in) and fairly accurate manufacturers' specifications for the sensors and effectors of the robot. Theoretically, I had enough knowledge to write correct program. However, the specifications

of the abilities of the robot and of the properties of the environment were impossible for me to translate directly into a working program. So, I worked in the following debugging cycle:

- Write a program for the robot;
- Run the program on the robot and watch it drive into a wall;
- Analyze the behavior of the robot and see where the program was mistaken;
- Fix the problem in the program;
- Run the program on the robot and watch it drive into a wall (this time for a different reason!);

and so on. The result of this cycle was that I learned a good deal about the nature of the interaction between the robot's sensors and the physical environment. Using this information, I *learned* about the environment and *adapted* the robot's behavior so that it would perform its task correctly. A much more efficient strategy would have been for me to design a behavior for the robot that would, *itself*, adapt to the environment it was in.

The need for adaptability is even more pronounced when the specification of the environment is quite weak, allowing for a variety of different types of environments or even environments whose characteristics change over time. In that case, no amount of off-line learning on the part of the designer will allow a correct fixed strategy to be obtained, because the correct behavior will vary from run to run and even from time to time during the course of a single run.

1.2 What Is Learning?

For the purposes of this discussion, let us take "learning" to mean, roughly, the improvement of a system's behavior by making it more appropriate for the environment in which the system is embedded. The term "learning" has been used for a much wider variety of processes, including so-called "symbol-level learning" [24] in which no information is gained, but the internal processes of the agent are made more efficient.

It is difficult to give a concrete computational definition for even this restricted form of learning. Many systems have internal state changes that are naturally termed "perception" rather than "learning." Consider a mobile robot that is programmed with a navigational strategy that is complete except for information about the width of the halls. The robot measures the width of the halls and begins to behave better because of having done so. Standard usage would say that the robot had "perceived" the width of the halls, and would not call this an instance of "learning." In common usage, "perception" tends to refer to gaining information that is specific, transient, or at a low level of abstraction, whereas "learning" tends to refer to more general information that is true over longer time spans. This issue is addressed in more detail in a paper comparing different views of the nature of knowledge [41]. In the rest of the book, this difficult question of the interpretation of natural language will be avoided completely; any instance of the improvement of behavior through increased information about the environment will be termed "learning."

1.3 What to Learn?

Having decided that the system must learn about its environment, we must decide exactly *what* the system is to learn.

In the end, the system must have some sort of operational mapping from perceptual states to effector actions. One approach is to learn this mapping directly from experience in the world. In this case, the action mapping is tailored for a particular task, so that if the task changes, an entirely new mapping must be learned. Having only a single task is not as restrictive as it may seem, however. For example, a robot might have the single task of carrying out orders given to it as it runs; these orders are perceived by the robot as indications about the state of the environment to which it must respond in a particular way.

Another approach would be to learn a more general model of the world. If the system could learn a description of the dynamics of the external environment, it would have enough information to satisfy any task within its physical abilities. In order to take action, however, it would need to have a description of its task and to use that description, together with the learned world model, to decide what to do. This process will, in many cases, reduce to the general planning problem, which has been shown to be intractable in the majority of cases [19]. Another option is to "compile" the world model and the task description into an action mapping that can be executed efficiently. If the task changes, the map need only be recompiled. This approach has been explored both in the case of user-supplied, symbolic world models [44] and in the case of learned world models [91]. In the first case, recompilation must be done all at once; in the second case, it is done incrementally.

Sutton [91] and Whitehead and Ballard [101] have found that in cases in which the reinforcement from the world is delayed, learning may be sped up by a kind of on-line compilation from a world model.

If the world model must be learned afresh, however, the results are inconclusive as to whether this method actually speeds up learning. In addition, this approach opens up the new and complex problem of learning world models, which has been addressed by a number of people, including Sutton and Pinette [92], Drescher [25], Mason, Christiansen, and Mitchell [54], Mel [56], Shen [85], and Lin [49].

For these reasons and because of the simplicity of the first method, this book will focus on techniques for learning action maps without building state-transition models as an intermediate stage. Even those methods that do use models have this simpler form of reinforcement learning as a component, so improved algorithms for learning action maps directly will benefit both approaches.

1.4 What to Learn from?

Whether the system is learning the action map directly or is learning a model of world dynamics as an intermediate stage, it must observe and glean information from the experience it has in the world. In addition to learning how the world works, the system must learn what its task is. It might somehow be possible to program this information in directly, but in general, that will defeat the purpose of the learning system. We will, instead, consider two second-order specifications that will cause the agent to learn to carry out a particular task in a particular environment.

One method is to provide a teacher, or other system, to emulate. We can then build our learning system with the fixed goal of coming to behave in the same way as the teacher, generating the same mapping from perceptual situations to effector actions, even when the teacher is no longer present to be observed.

Another method is to provide a "reinforcement signal"; this is essentially a mapping from each state of the environment into a scalar value encoding how desirable that state is for the agent. The system's goal, in this case, would be to take actions that maximize the reinforcement values received, possibly over a long term.

As a concrete example, consider a simple robot with two wheels and two photo-sensors. It can execute five different actions: stop, go forward, go backward, turn left, and turn right. It can sense three different states of the world: the light in the left eye is brighter than that in the right eye, the light in the right eye is brighter than that in the left eye, and the light in both eyes is roughly equally bright. Additionally, the robot is given high values of reinforcement when the average value of light in the two eyes is increased from the previous instant. In order to maximize its reinforcement, this robot should turn left when the light in its left eye is brighter, turn right when the light in its right eye is brighter, and move forward when the light in both eyes is equal. The problem of learning to act is to discover such a mapping from perceptual states to actions.

Thus, the problem of learning to act can be cast as a function-learning problem: the agent must learn a mapping from the situations in which it finds itself, represented by streams of input values, to the actions it can perform. In the simplest case, the mapping will be a pure function of the current input value, but in general it can have state, allowing the action taken at a particular time to depend on the entire stream of previous input values.

In the past few years there has been a great deal of work in the AI and theoretical computer science communities on the problem of learning pure Boolean-valued functions [38, 57, 64, 72, 95]. Unfortunately, this work is not directly relevant to the problem of learning from reinforcement because of the different settings of the problem. In the traditional function-learning work, often referred to in the AI community as "concept learning," a learning algorithm is presented with a set or series of input-output pairs that specify the correct output to be generated for that particular input. This setting allows for effective function learning, but differs from the situation of a system trying to learn from reinforcement. The system, finding itself in a particular input situation, must generate an action. It then receives a reinforcement value from the environment, indicating how valuable the current world state is. The system cannot, however, deduce the reinforcement value that would have resulted from executing any of its other actions. Also, if the environment is noisy, as it will be in general, just one instance of performing an action in a situation may not give an accurate picture of the reinforcement value of that action.

Reinforcement learning reduces to concept learning when the system has only two possible actions, the world generates Boolean reinforcement that depends only on the most recently taken action, there is exactly one action that generates the high reinforcement value in each situation, and there is no noise. In this case, from performing a particular action in a situation, the system can deduce that it was the correct action if it was positively reinforced; otherwise it can infer that the other action would have been correct.

The problem of learning action maps by trial and error is often referred to as *reinforcement learning* because of its similarity to models used in psychological studies of behavior-learning in humans and animals [29]. It is also referred to as "learning with a critic," in contrast to the "learning with a teacher" of traditional supervised concept-learning [104]. One of the most interesting facets of the reinforcement-learning problem is the tension between performing actions that are not well understood in order to gain information about their reinforcement value and performing actions that are expected to be good in order to increase overall reinforcement. If a system believes that a particular action works well in a certain situation, it must trade off performing that action against performing another one that it knows nothing about, in case the second action is even better than the first. Or, as Ashby [7] put it,

> The process of trial and error can thus be viewed from two very different points of view. On the one hand it can be regarded as simply an attempt at success; so that when it fails we give zero marks for success. From this point of view it is merely a second-rate way of getting to success. There is, however, the other point of view that gives it an altogether higher status, for the process may be playing the invaluable part of *gathering information*, information that is absolutely necessary if adaptation is to be successfully achieved.

The longer the time span over which the system will be acting, the more important it is for the agent to be acting on the basis of correct information. Acting to gain information may improve the expected long-term performance while causing short-term performance to decline.

Another important aspect of the reinforcement-learning problem is that the actions that a system performs influence the input situations in which it will find itself in the future. Rather than receiving an independently chosen set of input-output pairs, the system has some control over what inputs it will receive and complete control over what outputs will be generated in response. In addition to making it difficult to make distributional statements about the inputs to the system, this degree of control makes it possible for what seem like small "experiments" to cause the system to discover an entirely new part of its environment.

In this book, we will investigate methods for learning action maps from reinforcement. For the purposes of building embedded systems, it is much easier to provide a reinforcement function than it is to provide a teacher that will specify the correct action for every possible situation. It is important to notice, however, that we have not completely eliminated the problem of programming embedded systems; we have simply changed the nature of the program. Now, instead of specifying the action mapping directly, the designer must specify a reinforcement function, which tells the system which states of the world are desirable. By using reinforcement learning, some of the programming burden is lifted from the human and placed on the system, which is, after all, where it should be.

1.5 Representation

The question of knowledge representation has sparked a great deal of controversy within AI and related areas. Very often, the choice of representation of learned information directly influences the speed and abilities of the learning system. Possible representations of action maps vary widely and include tables, neural networks, first-order predicate calculus, and production rules. These representations can be grossly divided into statistical and symbolic methods.

Statistical learning methods encompass much of the early learning work in pattern recognition [71] and adaptive control [32], as well as current work in artificial neural networks (also known as connectionist systems) [10]. The internal representations used are typically numeric and the correctness of algorithms is demonstrated using statistical methods. These systems tend to be highly noise-tolerant and robust. However, the internal states are difficult for humans to interpret and the algorithms often perform poorly on discrete problems.

More symbolic approaches to learning, such as those standardly pursued in the artificial intelligence community, attempt to address these issues of understandability and complexity. They have resulted in algorithms, such as Mitchell's version spaces [63] and Michalski's STAR [57], that use easily interpretable symbolic representations and whose correctness hinges on arguments from logic rather than from statistics. These algorithms tend to suffer severely from noise intolerance and high computational complexity.

Many researchers use symbolic representations because, as Michie [59] puts it, "In AI-type learning, explainability is all." That is not the motivation for this work, which simply seeks the most effective algorithms for building embedded systems. There is, however, an important benefit of using symbolic representations of concepts and strategies being learned by an agent: it may allow the learned knowledge to be more easily integrated with knowledge that is provided by humans at design time. Although such integration is not explored in this book, it is an important direction in which learning research should be pursued.

One of the aims of the work in this book is to blend the statistical and the symbolic in algorithms for reinforcement learning in embedded systems. An important characteristic of most embedded systems is that they operate in environments that are not (to them) completely predictable. In order to work effectively in such environments, a system must be able to summarize general tendencies of its environment. The well-understood methods of statistics are most appropriate for this task. This does not, however, mean we must abandon all of the benefits of symbolic AI methods. Rather, these two approaches can be synthesized to make learning systems that are robust and noise-tolerant as well as being easy to understand and capable of working in complex discrete environments. A good example of this kind of synthesis is Quinlan's successful concept-learning method, ID3 [72]. Within the combined approach, complexity issues can be addressed by explicitly considering limited classes of functions to be learned.

We will explore a variety of representational strategies, with primary concern for the efficiency and effectiveness of using the representation rather than with general methodological preferences.

1.6 Situated Action

In the 1980s, many researchers in AI began to feel uncomfortable with the way the field was progressing. They saw a field that was fragmented, with individuals or groups studying perception, reasoning, learning, action, and language in almost complete isolation from one another. Each of these independent efforts was making its own assumptions about what it could depend on from the others; these assumptions were rarely grounded in any knowledge of the other enterprises.

From these observations arose the desire to construct entire agents that made the connection between perception and action while embedded or *situated* in dynamic environments. This integrated, situated approach has been pursued in different ways by a number of researchers, including Brooks [16], Agre and Chapman [1], and Rosenschein and Kaelbling [45].

The work in this book arises out of this tradition of situated action. The methods are all intended to work in the context of agents embedded in dynamic environments. The domains to which they have been applied so far have been quite simple, more at the level motor skills than of intellectual activity. These methods are not expected to be sufficient for tasks like playing chess, but they will help us gain the necessary understanding of routine interactions with the physical world before we go on to tackle higher level problems.

1.7 Theory and Practice

In the best of all possible worlds, we would invent complex algorithms, prove them to have desirable properties, and demonstrate them to be useful in empirical trials. In the real world, this is unfortunately quite difficult. In the case of reinforcement learning, the algorithms about which things can readily be proven are very simple and not particularly useful; algorithms that are useful are too complex to be analyzed theoretically.

This work is driven directly by the goal of having useful algorithms for reinforcement learning in embedded systems. Whenever some theoretical insight is available, we make use of it, but the discussion is not constrained to those properties of algorithms that can be established theoretically. There are extensive empirical results on the performance of reinforcement-learning algorithms; it would be wonderful if they inspired someone to do theoretical analysis of the algorithms, but if they do not, we must be content for now with methods that seem to work.

1.8 Contents

This book starts with a very simple formulation of the reinforcement-learning problem, then slowly adds complexity along different dimensions, providing previous work, new algorithms, and experimental results at each step along the way.

The first step is to understand the formal foundations of reinforcement learning. The foundations of this problem have been developed, largely independently, in the areas of statistics, dynamic programming, and learning-automata theory. By formalizing the problem of reinforcement learning, we can precisely characterize particular problem domains along different dimensions of complexity, including size of the input and output spaces, amount of noise, and the period of time over which behavior is to be optimized. Most importantly, the formalization will allow us to state objective criteria by which learning algorithms can be compared.

Having established a vocabulary for talking about environments and about the performance of learning methods within those environments, we survey existing algorithms for reinforcement learning from a variety of different literatures. We first consider methods for solving the "two-armed bandit" problem, which is the simplest possible setting of reinforcement learning. The system has only two actions available to it and all of the states of the world look the same, so an action strategy consists of a single action to be executed forever into the future. We then go on to consider associative forms of this problem, in which the system must learn to choose actions for different states of the world.

A new approach to the two-armed bandit problem, called the *interval estimation algorithm*, is presented in chapter 4. This algorithm uses second-order information about the reinforcement values to construct confidence-interval estimates of the value of performing the different actions. There is some theoretical discussion of the performance of the algorithm, followed by an empirical comparison to a wide variety of previously existing methods on a set of synthetic problems. The interval estimation method proves to have superior performance overall and shows an important lack of dependence on its internal parameters.

In the next chapter, we step back briefly and consider the following question: If we have a method for learning action maps that have only two actions, can we combine instances of that method to learn action maps with many actions? The question is answered in the affirmative by the *cascade method*, which requires N instances of the two-action learner to solve a problem with 2^N actions. The cascade method is shown to be correct, but convergence times are not addressed formally. Empirical trials show a cascaded version of the interval estimation method to converge faster than a more straightforward extension to multiple actions; this speed-up can be attributed to the parallelism of the multiple instances of the basic algorithm.

Armed with the ability to compose Boolean action maps into more complex ones, we now address the question of complexity of the input space. The interval estimation algorithm, when applied to a problem with multiple world states, simply makes a copy of itself for each possible state; this results in a space complexity exponential in the number of input bits and does not allow for any generalization across input instances. Chapters 6 and 7 each present algorithms for learning Boolean functions from reinforcement that have their statistical basis in the interval estimation method. By restricting the class of action maps that can possibly be learned, these methods *bias* the search for a good action map, gaining considerable time and space efficiency and allowing for generalization across input instances.

Previous work in computational learning theory has found the restriction to the class of functions describable as propositional formulae in k-DNF to provide a useful bias. Chapter 6 presents two algorithms for learning functions in k-DNF from reinforcement, one based on existing techniques of linear associators and the other based on the interval estimation method. Both of the new techniques prove to be empirically superior to previous methods on synthetic problems with a variety of characteristics.

A more flexible algorithm is presented in chapter 7. The GTRL algorithm performs a restricted, real-time, generate-and-test search in a syntactic space of Boolean-function descriptions. It uses statistical heuristics to guide the search; for a large class of target functions, these heuristics generate the correct answer almost immediately; for parity and related functions, the search may take considerably more steps. The algorithm is highly parameterized and can be given a weak or strong bias, making it more or less general and less or more efficient. The GTRL algorithm is tested on the problems from the previous chapter and is shown, on the most complex problem, to have the best performance, due to the direct guidance of the search heuristics.

An important problem with the preceding methods is that they assume that the system has the perceptual abilities to discriminate between states of the world in which one action must be taken and states of the world in which another action must be taken. In general, this will not be the case; states with important differences will appear the same to the system. This problem has been called *perceptual aliasing* [102] and has proven to be very difficult to address. A system can discriminate between more states of the world if it can remember its previous percepts. A simple solution to the problem of perceptual aliasing is simply to extend the system's inputs to include the last k percepts for some value of k. As k gets large, the input space grows dramatically, and we are again subject to the complexity problems we have been trying to avoid. Chapter 8 presents a novel attempt at addressing the problem of perceptual aliasing that does not increase the size of the input space and that allows actions to depend, potentially, on percepts that occurred arbitrarily far back in time. This new method, an extension of the GTRL algorithm, is shown to work on simple problems, but is not satisfactory as the problems become more complex. This will be an important area for future research.

All of the methods discussed so far have attempted choose an action that optimizes only the reinforcement received on the next step. In the more general case, actions should be chosen to optimize reinforcement into the future. This would allow a system to learn to take actions that have no immediate effect, but that generate high reinforcement values sometime after they have been executed. There are some very good existing techniques for handling delayed reinforcement; chapter 9 reviews these techniques, then extends them to incorporate the statistical ideas of the interval estimation method. The resulting algorithms are compared experimentally on difficult synthetic problems.

The algorithms presented in this book are finally validated through their application to moderately complex domains, including a real mobile robot. Chapter 10 describes these experiments, documenting their successes and failures.

There is a great deal of future work to be done in the area of reinforcement learning. One of the most pressing issues is the integration of learned knowledge with existing knowledge. In this book, we have considered only *tabula rasa* learning, and seen that it works fairly well on simple problems. Studying learning in isolation allows us to see clearly what the main difficulties are and to perform clean experimental tests of possible solutions. Learning will almost certainly not take us all the way to intelligent systems. We must eventually reintegrate learning with *a priori* knowledge, potentially in the form of existing structure. Understanding how to do this integration must be a high priority for any future work in this area.

Chapter 2

Foundations

This chapter focuses on building formal foundations for the problem of learning in embedded systems. These foundations must allow a clear statement of the problem and provide a basis for evaluating and comparing learning algorithms. It is important to establish such a basis: there are many instances in the machine learning literature of researchers doing interesting work on learning systems, but reporting the results using evaluation metrics that make it difficult to compare their results with the results of others. The foundational ideas presented in this chapter are a synthesis of previous work in statistics [13], dynamic programming [74], the theory of learning automata [69], and previous work on the foundations of reinforcement learning [9, 89, 90, 97, 106, 107].

2.1 Acting in a Complex World

An embedded system, or agent, can be seen as acting in a world, continually executing a procedure that maps the agent's perceptual inputs to its effector outputs. Its world, or environment, is everything that is outside the agent itself, possibly including other robotic agents or humans. The agent operates in a cycle, receiving an input from the world, performing some computation, then generating an output that affects the world. The mapping that it uses may have state or memory, allowing its action at any time to depend, potentially, on the entire stream of inputs that it has received until that time. Such a mapping from an input stream to an output stream is referred to as a *behavior.*

In order to study the effectiveness of particular behaviors, whether or not they involve learning, we must model the connection between agent and world, understanding how an agent's actions affect its world and, hence, its own input stream.

2.1.1 Modeling an Agent's Interaction with the World

The world can be modeled as a deterministic finite automaton whose state transitions depend on the actions of an agent [55]. From the agent's perspective, the world is everything that is not itself, including other agents and processes. This model will be extended to include nondeterministic worlds in the next section. A world can be formally modeled as the triple (S, A, W), in which

- S is the set of possible states of the world,
- A is the set of possible outputs from the agent to the world (or actions that can be performed by the agent), and
- W is the state transition function, mapping $S \times A$ into S.

Once the world has been fixed, the agent can be modeled as the 4-tuple $(\mathcal{I}, I, R, B)$ where

- $\mathcal{I}$ is the set of possible inputs from the world to the agent,
- I is a mapping from S to $\mathcal{I}$ that determines which input the agent will receive when the world is in a given state,
- R is the reinforcement function of the agent that maps S into real numbers (it will also be useful to consider more limited models in which the output of the reinforcement function is Boolean-valued), and
- B is the behavior of the agent, mapping $\mathcal{I}^*$ (streams of inputs) into A.

The expressions $i(t)$ and $a(t)$ will denote the input received by the agent at time t and the action taken by the agent at time t, respectively.

The process of an agent's interaction with the world is depicted in figure 1. The world is in some internal state, s, that is projected into i and r by the input and reinforcement functions I and R. These values

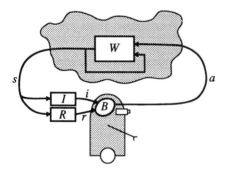

Figure 1
An agent's interaction with its world

serve as inputs to the agent's behavior, B, which generates an action a as output. Once per synchronous cycle of this system, the value of a, together with the old value of world state s, is transformed into a new value of world state s by the world's transition function W.

Note that if the agent does not have a simple stimulus-response behavior, but has some internal state, then the action taken by the behavior can be a function of both its input and its internal state. This internal state may allow the agent to discriminate among more states of the world and, hence, to obtain higher reinforcement values by performing more appropriate actions. To simplify the following discussion, actions will be conditioned only on the input, but the treatment can be extended to the case in which the action depends on the agent's internal state as well.

2.1.2 Inconsistent Worlds

One of the most difficult problems that an agent must contend with is apparent inconsistency. A world is said to be *apparently inconsistent* for an agent if it is possible that, on two different occasions in which the agent receives the same input and generates the same action, the next states of the world differ in their reinforcement or the world changes state in such a way that the same string of future actions will have different reinforcement results.

There are many different phenomena that can account for apparent inconsistency:

- *The agent does not have the ability to discriminate among all world states.* If the agent's input function I is not one-to-one, which will be the case in general, then an individual input could have arisen from many world states. When some of those states respond differently to different actions, the world will appear inconsistent to the agent.
- *The agent has "faulty" sensors.* Some percentage of the time, the world is in a state s, which should cause the agent to receive $I(s)$ as input, but it appears that the world is in some other state s', causing the agent to receive $I(s')$ as input instead. Along with the probability of error, the nature of the errors must be specified: are the erroneously perceived states chosen maliciously, or according to some distribution over the state space, or contingently upon what was to have been the correct input?
- *The agent has "faulty" effectors.* Some percentage of the time, the agent generates action a, but the world actually changes state as if the agent had generated a different action a'. As above, both the probability and nature of the errors must be specified.

- *The world has a probabilistic transition function.* In this case, the world is a stochastic automaton whose transition function, W', actually maps $S \times A$ into a probability distribution over S (a mapping from S into the interval $[0, 1]$ such that for every state s and action a, $\sum_{s' \in S} W'(s, a)(s') = 1$) that describes the probability that each of the states in S will be the next state of the world.

Some specific cases of the noise phenomena above have been studied in the formal function-learning literature. Valiant [95] has explored a model of noise in which, with some small probability, the entire input instance to the agent can be chosen maliciously. This corresponds, roughly, to having simultaneous faults in sensing and action that can be chosen in a way that is maximally bad for the learning algorithm. This model is overly pessimistic and is hard to justify in practical situations. Angluin [6] works with a model of noise in which input instances are misclassified with some probability; that is, the output part of an input-output pair is specified incorrectly. This is a more realistic model of noise, but is not directly applicable to the action-learning problem under consideration here.

If the behavior of faulty sensors and effectors is not malicious, the inconsistency they cause can be described by transforming the original world model into one in which the set of world states, S, is identical to the set of agent inputs, I, and in which the world has a probabilistic transition function. Inconsistency due to inability to discriminate among world states can also be modeled in this way, but such a model is correct only for the one-step transition probabilities of the system. Reducing each of these phenomena to probabilistic world-transition functions allows the rest of the discussion of embedded behaviors to ignore the other possible modes of inconsistency. The remainder of this section shows how to transform worlds with each type of inconsistency into worlds with state set I and probabilistic transition functions.

Consider an agent, embedded in a world with deterministic transition function W, whose effectors are faulty with probability ρ, so that when the intended action is a, the actual action is $\nu(a)$. This agent's situation can be described by a probabilistic world transition function $W'(s, a)$ that maps the value of $W(s, a)$ to the probability value $1 - \rho$, the value of $W(s, \nu(a))$ to the probability value ρ and all other states to probability value 0. That is,

$$W'(s, a)(W(s, a)) = 1 - \rho$$
$$W'(s, a)(W(s, \nu(a))) = \rho$$

The result of performing action a in state s will be $W(s,a)$ with probability $1 - \rho$, and $W(s, \nu(a))$ with probability ρ. Figure 2 depicts this transition function. First, a deterministic transition is made based on the action of the agent; then, a probabilistic transition is made by the world. This model can be easily extended to the case in which ν is a mapping from actions to probability distributions over actions. For all a' not equal to a, the value of $W(s, a')$ is mapped to the probability value $\rho\, \nu(a)(a')$, which is the probability, ρ, of an error times the probability that action a' will be executed given that the agent intended to execute the action a. The value of $W(s, a)$ is mapped to the probability value $1 - \rho + \rho\, \nu(a)(a)$, which is the probability that there is no error, plus the probability that the error actually maps back to the correct action.

Faulty input sensors are somewhat more difficult to model. Let the agent's sensors be faulty with probability ρ, yielding a value $I(\nu(s))$ rather than $I(s)$. We can construct a new model with a probabilistic world transition function in which the states of the world are those that the agent *thinks* it is in. The model can be most simply viewed if the world makes more than one probabilistic transition, as shown in figure 3. If it appears that the world is in state s, then with probability ρ_s, it actually is, and the first transition is to the same state. The rest of the probability mass is distributed over the other states in the inverse image of s under ν, $\nu^{-1}(s)$, causing a transition to some world state s' with probability $\rho_{s'}$. Next, there is a transition to a new state on the basis of the agent's action according to the original transition function W. Finally, with probability ρ, the world makes a transition to the state $\nu(W(s', a))$, allowing for the chance that this result will be misperceived on the next tick. In figure 4, the diagram of figure 3 is converted into a more standard form, in which the agent performs an action, and then the world makes a probabilistic transition. This construction can also be extended to the cases in which $\nu(s)$ is a probability distribution over S and in which the initial world transition function is probabilistic.

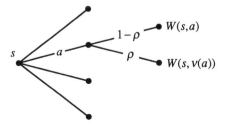

Figure 2
Modeling faulty effectors with a probabilistic world transition function

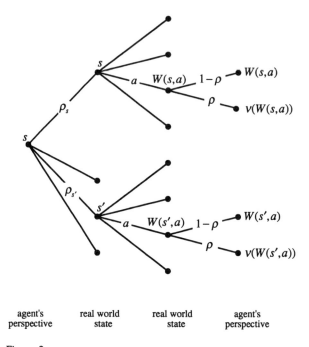

agent's   real world   real world   agent's
perspective   state   state   perspective

Figure 3
Modeling faulty sensors with multiple probabilistic transitions

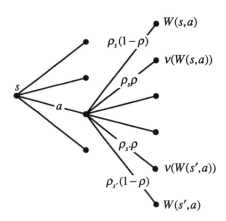

Figure 4
Modeling faulty sensors with a probabilistic world transition function

We can construct an approximate model of an agent's inability to discriminate among world states by creating a new model of the world in which the elements of $\mathcal{I}$ are the states, standing for equivalence classes of the states in the old model. Let $\{s_1, \ldots, s_n\}$ be the inverse image of i under I. There is a probabilistic transition to each of the s_j, based on the probability, ρ_j, that the world is in state s_j given that the agent received the input i. From each of these states, the world makes a transition on the basis of the agent's action, a, to the state $W(s_j, a)$, which is finally mapped back down to the new state space by the function I. This process is depicted in figure 5 and the resulting transition function is shown in figure 6. The new transition function gives a correct one-step model of the transition probabilities, but will not generate the same distribution of sequences of two or more states.

In the construction for faulty sensors, it is necessary to evaluate the probability that the world is in some state s_k, given that it appears to the agent to be in another state s. This probability depends on the unconditional probability that the world is in the state s_k, as well as the unconditional probability that the world appears to be in the state s. These unconditional probabilities depend, in the general case, on the behavior that the agent is executing, so the construction cannot be carried out before the behavior is fixed. A similar problem exists for the case of lack of discrimination: it is necessary to evaluate the probability that the world is in each of the individual states in the inverse image of input i under I given that the agent received input i. These probabilities also depend on the behavior that is being executed by the agent. This leads to a very complex optimization problem that is, in its general form, beyond the scope of this work.

This work will mainly address learning in worlds that are globally consistent for the learning agent. A world is *globally consistent* for an agent if and only if for all inputs $i \in \mathcal{I}$ and actions $a \in A$, the *expected* value of the reinforcement given i and a is constant. Global consistency allows for variations in the result of performing an action in a situation, as long as the expected, or average, result is the same. It simply requires that there not be variations in the world that are undetectable by the agent and that affect its choice of action. Important hidden state in the world can cause such variations; methods for learning to act in such worlds are discussed in chapter 7. If the transformation described above has been carried out so that the sets $\mathcal{I}$ and $\mathcal{S}$ are the same, the requirement for global consistency is tantamount to requiring that the resulting world be a Markov decision process with stationary transition and output probabilities [46]. In addition, the following discussion will assume that the world is consistent over changes in the agent's behavior.

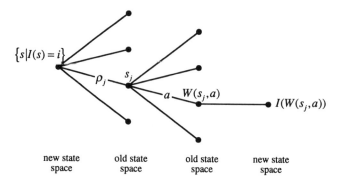

Figure 5
Modeling inability to discriminate among worlds

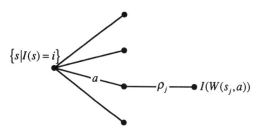

Figure 6
Modeling inability to discriminate among worlds with a probabilistic world transition function

2.1.3 Learning Behaviors

The problem of programming an agent to behave correctly in a world is to choose some behavior B, given that the rest of the parameters of the agent and world are fixed. If the programmer does not know everything about the world, or if he wishes the agent he is designing to be able to operate in a variety of different worlds, he must program an agent that will *learn to behave correctly*. That is, he must find a behavior that, through changing parts of its internal state on the basis of its perceptual stream, eventually converges to some behavior B' that is appropriate for the world that gave rise to its perceptions. Of course, to say that a program learns is just to take a particular perspective on a program with internal state. A behavior with state can be seen as "learning" if parts of its state eventually converge to some fixed or slowly varying values. The behavior that results from those parameters having been fixed in that way can be called the "learned behavior."

A *learning behavior* is an algorithm that learns an appropriate behavior for an agent in a world. It is itself a behavior, mapping elements of $\mathcal{I}$ to elements of $\mathcal{A}$, but it requires the additional input r, which designates the reinforcement value of the world state for the agent. A learning behavior consists of three parts: an initial state s_0, an update function u, and an evaluation function e.[1] At any moment, the internal state, s, encodes whatever information the learner has chosen to save about its interactions with the world. The update function maps an internal state of the learner, an input, an action, and a reinforcement value into a new internal state, adjusting the current state based on the reinforcement resulting from performing that action in that input situation. The evaluation function maps an internal state and an input into an action, choosing the action that seems most useful for the agent in that situation, based on the information about the world stored in the internal state. Recall that an action can be useful for an agent either because it has a high reinforcement value or because the agent knows little about its outcome. Figure 7 shows a schematic view of the internal structure of a learning behavior. The register s has initial value s_0 and can be thought of as programming the evaluation function e to act as a particular state-free action map. The update function, u, updates the value of s on each clock tick.

A general algorithm for learning behaviors, based on these three components, is shown in figure 8. The internal state is initialized to s_0, and then the algorithm loops forever. An input is read from the

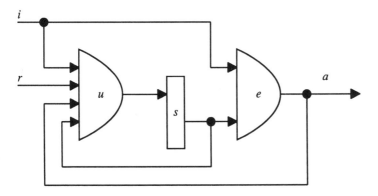

Figure 7
Decomposition of a learning behavior

[1]From this point on, the variable s will refer to an internal state of the learning behavior. Because we have assumed the transformations described in the previous section, it is no longer important to name the different states of the world.

```
s := s₀
loop
        i := input
        a := e(s, i)
        output a
        r := reinforcement
        s := u(s, i, a, r)
end loop
```

Figure 8
General algorithm for learning behaviors

world and the evaluation function is applied to the internal state and the input, resulting in an action, which is then output. At this point, the world makes a transition to a new state. The program next determines the reinforcement associated with the new world state, uses that information, together with the last input and action, to update the internal state, and then goes back to the top of its loop. Formulating learning behaviors in terms of s_0, e, and u facilitates building experimental frameworks that allow testing of different learning behaviors in a wide variety of real and simulated worlds.

2.2 Performance Criteria

In order to compare algorithms for learning behaviors, we must fix the criteria on which they are to be judged. There are three major considerations: correctness, convergence, and time-space complexity. First, we must determine the correct behavior for an agent in a domain. Then we can measure to what degree a learned behavior approximates the correct behavior and the speed, in terms of the number of interactions with the world, with which it converges. We must also be concerned with the amount of time and space needed for computing the update and evaluation functions and with the size of the internal state of the algorithm.

2.2.1 Correctness

When shall we say that a behavior is correct for an agent in an environment? There are many possible answers that will lead to different learning algorithms and analyses. An important quantity is the expected reinforcement that the agent will receive in the next instant, given that the current input is $i(t)$ and the current action is $a(t)$, which can be expressed as

$$er(i(t), a(t)) - E(R(i(t+1)) \mid i(t), a(t)) = \sum_{i' \in \mathcal{I}} R(i')W'(i(t), a(t))(i').$$

It is the sum, over all possible next world states, of the probability that the world will make a transition to that state times its reinforcement value. This formulation assumes that the inputs directly correspond to the states of the world and that W' is a probabilistic transition function. If the world is globally consistent for the agent, then the process is Markov and the times are irrelevant in the above definition, allowing it to be restated as

$$er(i, a) = \sum_{i' \in \mathcal{I}} R(i')W'(i, a)(i').$$

One of the simplest criteria is that a behavior is correct if, at each step, it performs the action that is expected to cause the highest reinforcement value to be received on the next step. A correct behavior, in this case, is one that generates actions that are optimal under the following definition:

$$\forall i \in \mathcal{I}, a \in \mathcal{A}. \, \mathrm{Opt}(i, a) \leftrightarrow \forall a' \in \mathcal{A}. \, er(i, a) \geq er(i, a').$$

Optimal behavior is defined as a relation on inputs and actions rather than as a function, because there may be many actions that are equally good for a given input. However, it can be made into a function by breaking ties arbitrarily. This is a local criterion that may cause the agent to sacrifice future reinforcement for immediately attainable current reinforcement.

The concept of expected reinforcement can be made more global by considering the total expected reinforcement for a finite future interval, or *horizon*, given that an action was taken in a particular input situation. This is often termed the *value* of an action, and it is computed with respect to a particular behavior (because the value of the next action taken depends crucially on how the agent will behave after that). In the following, expected reinforcement is computed under the assumption that the agent will act according to the optimal policy the rest of the time. The expected reinforcement, with horizon k, of doing action a in input situation i at time t is defined as

$$er_k(i(t), a(t))$$
$$= E\left(\sum_{j=1}^{k} R(i(t+j)) \mid i(t), a(t), \forall h < k. \, \mathrm{Opt}_{k-h}(i(t+h), a(t+h))\right).$$

This expression can be simplified to a recursive, time-independent formulation, in which the k-step value of an action in a state is just the one-step value of the action in the state plus the expected $k-1$-step value of the optimal action for horizon $k - 1$ in the following state:

$$er_k(i, a) = er(i, a) + \sum_{i' \in \mathcal{I}} W'(i, a)(i')\, er_{k-1}(i', \mathrm{Opt}_{k-1}(i')).$$

This definition is recursively dependent on the definition of optimality k steps into the future, Opt_k:

$$\forall i \in \mathcal{I}, a \in \mathcal{A}.\ \mathrm{Opt}_k(i, a) \leftrightarrow \forall a' \in \mathcal{A}.\ er_k(i, a) \geq er_k(i, a').$$

The values of er_1 and Opt_1 are just er and Opt given above. The k-step value of action a in situation i at time t, $er_k(i, a)$, can be computed by dynamic programming [13]. First, the Opt_1 relation is computed; this allows the er_2 function to be calculated for all i and a. Proceeding for k steps will generate the value for er_k. Because of the assumption that the world is Markov, these values are not dependent on the time. However, if k is large, the computational expense of this method is prohibitive.

Another way to define global optimality is to consider an infinite sum of future reinforcement values, in which near term values are weighted more heavily than values to be received in the distant future. This is referred to as a *discounted* sum, depending on the parameter γ to specify the rate of discounting. *Expected discounted reinforcement* at time t is defined as

$$er_\gamma(i(t), a(t))$$

$$= E\left(\sum_{j=1}^{\infty} \gamma^{j-1} R(i(t + j)) \mid i(t), a(t), \forall h > 0.\ \mathrm{Opt}_\gamma(i(t + h), a(t + h)) \right).$$

Properties of the exponential allow us to reduce this expression to

$$er(i(t), a(t)) + \gamma er_\gamma(i(t + 1), a(t + 1)),$$

which can be expressed independent of time as

$$er_\gamma(i, a) = er(i, a) + \gamma \sum_{i' \in \mathcal{I}} W'(i, a)(i')\, er_\gamma(i', \mathrm{Opt}_\gamma(i')).$$

The related definition of γ-discounted optimality is given by

$$\forall i \in \mathcal{I}, a \in \mathcal{A}.\ \mathrm{Opt}_\gamma(i, a) \leftrightarrow \forall a' \in \mathcal{A}.\ er_\gamma(i, a) \geq er_\gamma(i, a').$$

For a given value of γ and a proposed definition of Opt_γ, er_γ can be found by solving a system of equations, one for each possible instantiation of its arguments. A dynamic programming method called *policy iteration* [74] can be used in conjunction with that solution method to adjust policy Opt_γ until it is truly the optimal behavior. This definition of optimality is more widely used than finite-horizon optimality because its exponential form makes it more computationally tractable. It is also an intuitively satisfying model, with slowly diminishing importance attached to events in the distant future.

As an illustration of these different measures of optimality, consider the world depicted in figure 9. In state A, the agent has a choice as to whether to go right or left; in all other states the world transition is the same no matter what the agent does. In the left loop, the only reinforcement comes at the last state before state A, but it has value 6. In the right loop, each state has reinforcement value 1. Thus, the average reinforcement is higher around the left loop, but it comes sooner around the right loop. The agent must decide what action to take in state A. Different definitions of optimality lead to different choices of optimal action.

Under the local definition of optimality, we have $er(A, L) = 0$ and $er(A, R) = 1$. The expected return of going left is 0 and of going right is 1, so the optimal action would be to go right.

Using the finite-horizon definition of optimality, which action is optimal depends on the horizon. For very short horizons, it is clearly better to go right. When the horizon, k, is 5, it becomes better to go left. A general rule for optimal behavior is that when in state A, if the horizon is 5 or more, go left, otherwise go right. Figure 10 shows a plot of the values of going left (solid line) and going right (dashed line) initially, assuming that all choices are made optimally thereafter. We can see that going right is initially best, but it is dominated by going left for all $k \geq 5$.

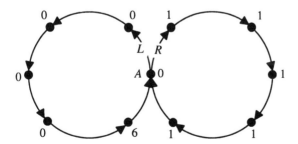

Figure 9

A sample deterministic world. The numbers represent the immediate reinforcement values that the agent will receive when it is in each of the states. The only choice of action is in state A.

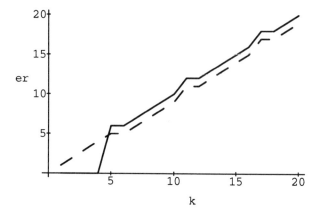

Figure 10
Plot of expected reinforcement against horizon k. Solid line indicates strategy of going left first, then behaving optimally. Dashed line indicates strategy of going right first, then behaving optimally.

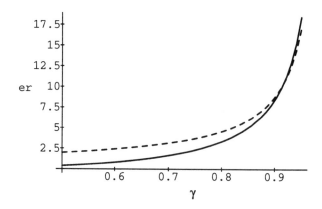

Figure 11
Plot of expected reinforcement against discount factor γ. Solid line indicates strategy of always going left. Dashed line indicates strategy of always going right.

Finally, we can consider discounted expected value. Figure 11 shows a plot of the expected reinforcement of the strategies of always going left at state A (solid line) and always going right at state A (dashed line) plotted as a function of γ. When there is a great deal of discounting (γ is small), it is best to go right because the reward happens sooner. As γ increases, going left becomes better, and at approximately $\gamma = 0.915$, going left dominates going right.

Using a global optimality criterion can require agents to learn that chains of actions will result in states with high reinforcement value. In such situations, the agent takes actions not because they directly result in good states, but because they result in states that are closer to the states with high payoff. One way to design learning behaviors that attempt to achieve these difficult kinds of global optimality is to divide the problem into two parts: transducing the global reinforcement signal into a local reinforcement signal and learning to perform the locally best action. The global reinforcement signal is the stream of values of $R(i(t))$ that come from the environment. The optimal local reinforcement signal, $\hat{R}(i(t))$, can be defined as $R(i(t)) + \gamma er_\gamma(i(t), \text{Opt}_\gamma(i(t))$. It is the value of the state $i(t)$ assuming that the agent acts optimally. As shown by Sutton [89], this signal can be approximated by the value of the state $i(t)$ given that the agent follows the policy it is currently executing. Sutton's adaptive heuristic critic (AHC) algorithm, an instance of the general class of temporal difference methods, provides a way of learning to generate the local reinforcement signal from the global reinforcement signal in such a way that, if combined with a correct local learning algorithm, it will converge to the true optimal local reinforcement values [89, 90]. A complication introduced by this method is that, from the local behavior-learner's point of view, the world is not stationary. This is because it takes time for the AHC algorithm to converge and because changes in the behavior cause changes in the values of states and therefore in the local reinforcement function. This and related methods will be explored further in chapter 8.

The following discussion will be in terms of some definition of the optimality of an action for a situation, $\text{Opt}(i, a)$, which can be defined in any of the three ways above, or in some novel way that is more appropriate for the domain in which a particular agent is working.

2.2.2 Convergence

Correctness is a binary criterion: either a behavior is or is not correct for its world. Since correctness requires that the behavior perform the optimal actions from the outset, it is unlikely that any "learning" behavior will ever be correct. Using a definition of correctness as a reference, however, it is possible to develop other measures of how close particular behaviors come to the optimal behavior. This section will consider two different classes of methods for characterizing how good or useful a behavior is in terms of its relation to the optimal behavior.

Classical Convergence Measures   Early work in the theory of machine learning was largely concerned with *learning in the limit* [14, 34]. A behavior converges to the optimal behavior in the limit if there is some time after which every action taken by the behavior is the same as the action that would have been taken by the optimal behavior.

Work in learning-automata theory has relaxed the requirements of learning in the limit by applying different definitions of probabilistic convergence to the sequence of internal states of a learning automaton. Following Narendra and Thathachar [69], the definitions are presented here. A learning automaton is said to be *expedient* if

$$\lim_{n \to \infty} E[M(n)] < M_0 \ ,$$

where $M(n)$ is the average penalty (they are trying to minimize "penalty" rather than maximize "reinforcement"—merely a terminological difference) for the internal state at time step n and M_0 is $M(n)$ for the pure-chance automaton that selects each action randomly with a uniform distribution. A learning automaton is said to be *optimal* if

$$\lim_{n \to \infty} E[M(n)] = c_l \ ,$$

where $c_l = min_i\{c_i\}$ and c_i is the expected penalty of executing action i. A learning automaton is said to be ϵ-*optimal* if

$$\lim_{n \to \infty} E[M(n)] < c_l + \epsilon$$

can be obtained for any arbitrary $\epsilon > 0$ by a proper choice of the parameters of the automaton. Finally, a learning automaton is said to be *absolutely expedient* if

$$E[M(n+1) \mid s(n)] < M(n)$$

for all legal internal states of the algorithm $s(n)$ and for all possible sets $\{c_i\}(i = 1, 2, \ldots, r)$ (under the assumption that environments with all expected penalties equal are excluded).

An important recent theoretical development is a model of Boolean-function learning algorithms that are *probably approximately correct* (PAC) [6, 95], that is, that have a high probability of converging to a function that closely approximates the optimal function. The correctness of a function is measured with respect to a fixed probability distribution on the input instances—a function is said to approximate another function to degree ϵ if the probability that they will disagree on any instance chosen according to the given probability distribution is less than ϵ. This model requires that there be a fixed distribution over the input instances and that each input to the algorithm be drawn according to that distribution.

For an agent to act effectively in the world, its inputs must provide some information about the state that the world is in. In general, when the agent performs an action it will bring about a change in the state of the world and, hence, a change in the information the agent receives about the world. Thus, it will be very unlikely that such an agent's inputs could be modeled as being drawn from a fixed distribution, making PAC-convergence an inappropriate model for autonomous agents.

In addition, the PAC-learning model is distribution-independent— it seeks to make statements about the performance of algorithms no matter how the input instances are distributed. As Buntine has pointed out [17], its predictions are often overly conservative for situations in which there is *a priori* information about the distribution of the input instances, or even in which certain properties of the actual sample, such as how many distinct elements it contains, are known.

Measuring Error over an Agent's Lifetime   None of the classical convergence measures take into account the behavior of the agent during the period in which it converges. Instead, they make what is, for an agent embedded in the world, an artificial distinction between a learning phase and an acting phase. Autonomous agents that have extended run times will be expected to learn for their entire lifetime. Because they may not encounter certain parts or aspects of their environments until arbitrarily late in the run, it is inappropriate to require all mistakes to be made before some fixed deadline.

Another way of characterizing the performance of a function-learning algorithm is to count the divergences it makes from the optimal function. Littlestone [51] has investigated this model extensively, characterizing the optimal number of "mistakes" for a Boolean-function learner and presenting algorithms that perform very well, under this measure, on certain classes of Boolean functions. This model is intuitively pleasing, making no restrictive division into learning and acting phases, but it is not presented as being suited to noisy or inconsistent domains. However, by assimilating the inconsistency of the domain into the definition of the target function, as in the requirement for optimal behavior, Opt, we can make use of mistake bounds in inconsistent domains. A behavior is said to make an *avoidable mistake* if, given some input instance i, it generates action a and $Opt(i, a)$ does not hold; that is, there was some other action that would have had a higher expected reinforcement.

Avoidable mistake bounds take into account the fact that many mistakes cannot be avoided by an agent with limited sensory abilities and unreliable effectors. However, this measure is not entirely appropriate, because every nonoptimal choice of action is considered to be a mistake of the same magnitude. The expected error of an action a given an input i, $err(a, i)$, is defined to be

$$err(a, i) = er(a', i) - er(a, i) \; ,$$

in which a' is any action such that $opt(a', i)$. The expected error associated with an optimal action is 0; for a nonoptimal action, it is just the decrease in expected reinforcement due to having executed that action rather than an optimal one. The error of a behavior, either in the limit, or for runs of finite length, can be measured by summing the errors of the actions it generates. This value, referred to in the statistics literature as the *regret* of a strategy [13], represents the expected amount of reinforcement lost due to executing this behavior rather than an optimal one. This is an appropriate performance metric for agents embedded in inconsistent environments because it measures expected loss of reinforcement, which is precisely what we would like to minimize in our agents.

In many situations, the optimal behavior is unknown or difficult to compute, which makes it difficult to calculate the error of a given behavior. It is still possible to use this measure to compare two different behaviors for the same agent and environment. The expected reinforcement for an algorithm over some time period can be estimated by running it several times and averaging the resulting total reinforcements. Because expectations are additive, the difference between the expected errors of two algorithms is the same as the difference between their expected total reinforcement values. Thus, the difference between average reinforcements is a valid measure of a behavior's correctness that is independent of the internal architecture of the algorithm and that can be used to compare results across a wide variety of techniques.

2.2.3 *Time and Space Complexity*

Autonomous agents must operate in the real world, continually receiving inputs from and performing actions on their environments. Because the world changes dynamically, an autonomous agent must be *reactive*—always aware of and reacting to changes in its environment. To ensure reactivity, an agent must operate in *real-time*; that is, its sense-compute-act cycle must keep pace with the unfolding of important events in the environment. The exact constraints on the reaction time of an agent are often difficult to articulate, but it is clear that, in general, unbounded computation must never take place.

A convenient way to guarantee real-time performance is to require that the behavior spend only a constant amount of time, referred to as a "tick," generating an action in response to each input. If the behavior is a learning behavior, the learning process must also spend only a constant amount of time on each input instance. There are two strategies for designing such a learning system: incremental and batch.

An incremental system processes each new data set or learning instance as it arrives as input. The processing must be efficient enough that the system is always ready for new data when it arrives. If new relevant data can arrive every tick, the learning algorithm must spend only one constant tick's worth of time on each instance. The requirement for incrementality can, theoretically, be relaxed to yield a batch system, in which a number of learning instances are collected, then processed for many ticks. As long as the learning system adheres to the tick discipline, this process need not interfere with the reactiveness of the rest of the system. Working in batch mode may limit the usefulness of the learning system to some degree, however, because the system will be working with old data that may not reflect the current situation and it will force the data that arrive during the computation phase to be ignored. When using this method, the input data must be sampled with care, in order to avoid statistical distributions of inputs that do not reflect those of the external world.

An algorithm can be said to be *strictly incremental* if it uses a bounded amount of time and space throughout its entire lifetime. This is in contrast with such approaches as Aha and Kibler's instance-based learning [2], which is incremental in that it processes one instance at a time, but is not strictly incremental because instances are stored in a memory whose size may increase without bound. For an incremental system that processes one instance per tick to perform in real time, the system must be strictly incremental.

By definition, the amount of time a strictly incremental behavior spends on each input does not vary as a function of the number of inputs that have been received. It will, however, depend on the size of the input and the output, but that is fixed at design time. This allows the programmer to know how long each tick of the learning behavior will take to compute on the available hardware and to compare that rate with the pace of events in the world.

Any formalization of the interaction between an agent and its world will depend on the rate of the interaction; behaviors that work at different rates will essentially be working in different environments. The expected values of optimal behaviors for different reaction rates will be quite different. In general, up to some minimum value, the faster an agent can interact with the world, the better (otherwise the agent does not have time to avert impending bad events), so we should strive for the most efficient algorithms possible, although a slow algorithm with better convergence properties might be preferable to a fast algorithm that is far from optimal.

Complex agents, such as mobile robots with a wide variety of sensors and effectors, will have a huge number of possible inputs and outputs. If algorithms for these agents are to be practical, they must have time and space complexity that is at worst polynomial in the number of input bits, $\lg(|\mathcal{I}|)$, and the number of output bits, $\lg(|\mathcal{A}|)$, rather than the number of inputs and outputs. As we shall see in section 4.6, this will only be achievable, in general, by limiting the class of behaviors that can be learned by the agent.

2.3 Related Foundational Work

The problem of learning the structure of a finite-state automaton from examples has been studied by many theoreticians, including Moore [67], Gold [35] and, more recently, Rivest and Schapire [73]. This is a very difficult problem that has only been studied in the case of deterministic automata. If the entire structure of the world can be learned, it is conceptually straightforward to compute the optimal behavior. It is important to note, however, that learning an action-map that maximizes reinforcement is likely to be much less complex than learning the world's transition function.

Watkins [97] presents a clear discussion of different types of optimality from an operations-research perspective and characterizes possible algorithms for learning optimal behavior from delayed rewards. Sutton [89, 90] shows how to divide the problem of learning from delayed reinforcement into the problems of locally optimal behavior learning and secondary reinforcement-signal learning. The implications of these ideas for learning from delayed reinforcement will be explored further in chapter 8.

Williams has done important work on the foundations of reinforcement learning, which is considerably different than the framework provided in this chapter [106, 107]. He has developed a general form for expressing reinforcement algorithms in which a wide variety of existing reinforcement learning algorithms may be described. In addition, he has shown that the algorithms expressed in this form are performing a gradient ascent search, in which the average update of the internal parameters of the algorithm is in the direction of steepest ascent for expected reinforcement.

Chapter 3

Previous Approaches

The problem of learning from reinforcement has been studied by a variety of researchers: statisticians studying the "two-armed bandit" problem, psychologists working on mathematical learning theory, learning-automata theorists, and researchers in artificial intelligence. This chapter explores the differing frameworks in which these groups have studied reinforcement learning and presents a few important algorithms and results from each area. It discusses previous approaches only to the simple reinforcement-learning scenario in which all reinforcement is instantaneous (the goal is to optimize local, immediate reinforcement) and the action maps to be learned are pure functions. As these assumptions are relaxed, in later chapters, other relevant work pertaining to the more complex situations will be discussed.

3.1 Bandit Problems

The reinforcement learning problem is addressed within the statistics community as the "two-armed bandit" problem: given a machine with two levers that independently pays some amount of money each time a lever is pulled, develop a strategy that gains the maximum payoff over time by choosing which lever to pull based on the previous experience of lever-pulling and payoffs. Among the early results was that the "stick with a winner but switch on a loser" strategy (that is, keep pulling a lever until it loses, then switch to the other one and keep pulling it until it loses, etc.) is expedient (better than choosing levers at random), but not optimal [13].

Most of the technical results in this area make very strict assumptions about the *a priori* information the player has about the probabilistic models underlying the payoff distributions of the two arms. These results may be useful in restricted situations, but are not applicable to the general problem of building learning agents.

There has been some consideration, however, of the *minimax* case, in which it is assumed that the events of arm-pulling are independent, that they pay off either nothing or a fixed amount, that the probability of each arm paying off remains constant for the entire game, and that the world will choose the probabilities in the way that is worst for the player. It has been shown [13] that the best possible strategy for such a domain has regret proportional to $(1 - \gamma)^{-1/2}$ for discounting factor γ and to $n^{1/2}$ for finite horizon n.

An example algorithm satisfying these requirements is formally described in algorithm 1.[1] The algorithm alternates between the two arms, keeping track of the number of successes of each. When the number of successes of one arm exceeds the number of successes of the other by k, it chooses the winning arm forever into the future. The array c contains counts of the number of successes of each arm; d encodes the decision about future actions; if it has value -1, the decision has not yet been made; l encodes the last action taken so that the algorithm can alternate between actions in the pre-decision phase. If reinforcement is to be optimized over a fixed horizon n, the parameter k should be chosen to be $n^{1/2}$. If reinforcement with discounting factor γ is to be optimized, k should be chosen to be $(1 - \gamma)^{-1/2}$. This is a simple algorithm with an upper bound on regret of $(1 - \gamma)^{-1/2}\left(1 + \frac{1}{2e}\right)$

The initial state, s_0, consists of 3 components: c, an array with two integer elements, and integers d and l. Initially, c contains zeros, $d = -1$, and $l = 0$.

$$u(s, a, r) = \quad \text{if } d = -1 \text{ then}$$
$$c[a] := c[a] + 1$$
$$e(s) = \quad \text{if } d = -1 \text{ then}$$
$$\text{if } c[0] - c[1] > k \text{ then begin}$$
$$d := 0; \text{ return } 0; \text{ end}$$
$$\text{else if } c[1] - c[0] > k \text{ then begin}$$
$$d := 1; \text{ return } 1; \text{ end}$$
$$\text{else if } l = 0 \text{ then begin}$$
$$l := 1; \text{ return } 1; \text{ end}$$
$$\text{else begin}$$
$$l := 0; \text{ return } 0; \text{ end}$$
$$\text{else return } d$$

Algorithm 1

The BANDIT algorithm

[1]There is no input argument, i, to the update and evaluation functions. This algorithm, as well as most of the others in the first part of the chapter, makes a choice about what action to perform for every future time step, independent of the state of the world, with only reinforcement as input.

in the discounted case or $(1 - n^{-1})^{-(n-1)} n^{1/2} \left(1 + \frac{1}{2e}\right)$ in the finite horizon case. This value is itself bounded above by $n^{1/2}(e + 1/2)$. In both
cases, the upper bound on regret is within a constant factor of optimal.
However, as we will see in section 4.4, this algorithm is outperformed
by many others in empirical tests.

In more recent work on the bandit problem, Lai [47] has developed an algorithm for finite horizon problems and has shown it to
be asymptotically optimal as the horizon approaches infinity. The algorithm has also been shown, empirically, to work well for small
horizons. Assuming the reinforcements for each arm come from a
univariate distribution, it constructs upper confidence bounds on the
parameters of the distribution of each arm and chooses the action with
the highest upper confidence bound. The bounds are based on results
from boundary crossing theory. In many cases of interest, including
the case of Bernoulli payoffs, a good closed-form approximation for
the bound is not known. The algorithm can be implemented using
iterative root-finding methods at each evaluation step, but it is not
completely satisfactory, because the amount of time taken per step is
not bounded.

3.2 Learning Automata

Another closely related field is that of learning automata. The phrase
"learning automata" means, in this case, automata that learn to act
in the world, as opposed to automata that learn the state-transition
structures of other automata (as in Moore [67]).

3.2.1 Early Work

The first work in this area took place in the Soviet Union. An example
of early learning-automaton work is the *Tsetlin automaton*, designed
by M. L. Tsetlin [94]. The input set of the automaton is $\{0, 1\}$, with
1 corresponding to the case when the agent receives reinforcement
and 0 corresponding to the case when it does not. As in the BANDIT
algorithm, there is no input corresponding to i, the information about
the state of the world. The automaton has two possible actions, or
outputs: 0 and 1. The operation of the Tsetlin automaton is described
in algorithm 2.

The Tsetlin automaton is parametrizable by the number, N, of states
between the center state and the ends of the chains going to the right
and left. It can be shown that, if one of the actions has success probability greater than .5, then, as the value N approaches infinity, the average
reinforcement approaches the maximum success probability [69].

The initial state can be any of the states, but would most reasonably be chosen to be state N or state $2N$. All of the states on the left half of the graph evaluate to action 0 and on the right half of the graph to action 1. The state update operation consists of making one of the labeled transitions: when reinforcement has value 1, a transition to the left is taken if the action was 0 and to the right if the action was 1; when the reinforcement has value 0, a right transition is taken if the action was 0 and a left transition if the action was 1. Zero reinforcement values move the state toward the center and positive reinforcement values move the state toward the end corresponding to the action that was taken.

Algorithm 2
The TSETLIN algorithm

There are many other similar learning automata, some with better convergence properties than this one. The BANDIT algorithm can also be easily modeled as a finite-state machine.

3.2.2 Probability-Vector Approaches

As it is difficult to conceive of complex algorithms in terms of finite-state transition diagrams, the learning automata community moved to a new model, in which the internal state of the learning algorithm is represented as a vector of nonnegative numbers that sum to 1. The length of the vector corresponds to the number of possible actions of the agent. The agent chooses an action probabilistically, with the probability that it chooses the nth action equal to the nth element of the state vector. The problem, then, is one of updating the values in the state vector depending on the most recent action and its outcome.

These and similar, related models were also independently developed by the mathematical psychology community [18] as models for human and animal learning.

The initial state, s_0, consists of p_1 and p_2, two positive real numbers such that $p_1 + p_2 = 1$.

$$u(s, a, r) = \quad \text{if a = 0 then}$$

            if $r = 0$ then
$$p_0 := (1 - \beta)p_0$$
              else $p_0 := p_0 + \alpha(1 - p_0)$

      else

            if $r = 0$ then
$$p_0 := p_0 + \beta(1 - p_0)$$
              else $p_0 := (1 - \alpha)p_0$

            $p_1 := 1 - p_0$

$$e(s) = \quad \left\{ \begin{array}{l} 0 \text{ with probability } p_0 \\ 1 \text{ with probability } p_1 \end{array} \right.$$

where $0 < \alpha, \beta < 1$.

Algorithm 3
The linear reward-penalty (L_{RP}) algorithm

Any instance of Algorithm L_{RP} in which $\beta = 0$.

Algorithm 4
The linear reward-inaction (L_{RI}) algorithm

The most common of these approaches, called the *linear reward-penalty* algorithm, is shown in algorithm 3. Whenever an action is chosen and succeeds, the probability of performing that action is increased in proportion to 1 minus its current probability; when an action is chosen and fails, the probability of performing the other action is increased in proportion to its current probability. The parameters α and β govern the amount of adjustment upon success and failure, respectively. An important specialization is the *linear reward-inaction* algorithm, described in algorithm 4, in which no adjustment is made to the probability vector when reinforcement value 0 is received.

The linear reward-penalty algorithm has asymptotic performance that is better than random (that is, it is expedient), but it is not optimal. It has no absorbing states, so it always executes the wrong action with some nonzero probability. The linear reward-inaction algorithm, on the other hand, has the absorbing states [1,0] and [0,1], because a probability is only ever increased if the corresponding action is taken and it succeeds. Once one of the probabilities goes to 0, that action will never be taken, so its probability can never be increased. The linear reward-inaction algorithm is ϵ-optimal; that is, the parameter α can be chosen in order to make the probability of converging to the wrong absorbing state as small as desired. As the value of α is decreased, the probability of converging to the wrong state is decreased; however, the rate of convergence is also decreased. Theoreticians have been unable to derive a general formula that describes the probability of convergence to the wrong state as a function of α and the initial value of p_1. This would be necessary in order to choose α to optimize reinforcement for runs of a certain length or with a certain discounting factor, as we did with k in the BANDIT algorithm above.

In addition to these linear approaches, a wide range of non-linear approaches have been proposed. One of the most promising is Thathachar and Sastry's method [93]. It is slightly divergent in form from the previous algorithms in that it keeps more state than simply the vector $\mathbf{p}$ of action probabilities. In addition, there is a vector $\hat{\mathbf{d}}$ of estimates of the expected reinforcements of executing each action. Reinforcement values are assumed to be real values in the interval [0,1]. A simple two-action version of this algorithm is shown in algorithm 5.

The R_j are the summed reinforcement values for each action, the Z_j are the number of times each action has been tried, and the $\hat{d}_j$ are the average reinforcement values for each action. The adjustment to the probability vector depends on the values of the $\hat{d}_j$ rather than on the direct results of recent actions. This introduces a damping effect, because as long as, for instance, $\hat{d}_0 > \hat{d}_1$, p_0 will be increased, even if it has a few negative-reinforcement results during that time.

The TS algorithm converges much faster than the linear algorithms L_{RP} and L_{RI}. One of the reasons may be that it naturally takes big steps in the parameter space when the actions are well differentiated (the difference between $\hat{d}_0$ and $\hat{d}_1$ is large) and small steps when they are not. It has been shown that, for any stationary random environment, there is some value of λ such that $p_l(n) \rightarrow 1$ in probability[2] as $n \rightarrow \infty$, where $p_l(n)$ is the probability of executing the action that has the highest expected reinforcement [93].

Although there are asymptotic convergence results for the learning automata methods, there has been no formal characterization of their regret.

---

[2]According to Narendra and Thathachar [69], "The sequence $\{X_n\}$ of random variables converges in probability to the random variable X if for every $\epsilon > 0$, $\lim_{n\to\infty} \Pr \{|X_n - X| \geq \epsilon\} = 0$."

The initial state, s_0, consists of the following 6 components: p_0 and p_1, which are positive real numbers such that $p_0 + p_1 = 1$, and $R_0 = R_1 = Z_0 = Z_1 = 0$.

$$u(s, a, r) = \quad \hat{d}_0 := R_0/Z_0; \; \hat{d}_1 := R_1/Z_1$$

if $a = 0$ then begin

    if $\hat{d}_0 > \hat{d}_1$ then

$$p_0 := p_0 + \lambda(\hat{d}_0 - \hat{d}_1)p_1$$

    else $p_0 := p_0 + \lambda(\hat{d}_0 - \hat{d}_1)p_0^2$

$$p_1 := 1 - p_0$$
$$R_0 := R_0 + r$$
$$Z_0 := Z_0 + 1$$

end else begin

    if $\hat{d}_1 > \hat{d}_0$ then

$$p_1 := p_1 + \lambda(\hat{d}_1 - \hat{d}_0)p_0$$

    else $p_1 := p_1 + \lambda(\hat{d}_1 - \hat{d}_0)p_1^2$

$$p_0 := 1 - p_1$$
$$R_1 := R_1 + r$$
$$Z_1 := Z_1 + 1$$

end

$$e(s) = \quad \begin{cases} 0 \text{ with probability } p_0 \\ 1 \text{ with probability } p_1 \end{cases}$$

where $0 < \lambda < 1$ is a positive constant.

Algorithm 5
The TS algorithm

3.3 Reinforcement-Comparison Methods

One drawback of most of the algorithms that have been presented so far is that reinforcement values of 0 and 1 cause the same sized adjustment to the internal state independent of the *expected* reinforcement value. Sutton [89] addressed this problem with a new class of algorithms, called *reinforcement-comparison* methods. These methods work by estimating the expected reinforcement, then adjusting the internal parameters of the algorithm proportional to the difference between the actual and estimated reinforcement values. Thus, in an environment that tends to generate reinforcement value 1 quite frequently, receiving the value 1 will cause less adjustment than will be caused by receiving the value 0.

An instance of the reinforcement-comparison method is shown in algorithm 6. The internal state consists of the "weight" w, which is

The internal state, s_0, consists of the values $w = 0$ and p, which will be initialized to the first reinforcement value received.

$$u(s, a, r) = \qquad \begin{aligned} w &:= w + \alpha(r - p)(a - 1/2) \\ p &:= p + \beta(r - p) \end{aligned}$$

$$e(s) = \qquad \begin{cases} 1 & \text{if } w + \nu > 0 \\ 0 & \text{otherwise} \end{cases}$$

where $\alpha > 0$, $0 < \beta < 1$, and ν is a normally distributed random variable of mean 0 and standard deviation δ_y.

Algorithm 6
A reinforcement-comparison (RC) algorithm

initialized to 0, and the predicted expected reinforcement, p, which is initialized to the first reinforcement value received. The output, $e(s)$, has value 1 or 0 depending on the values of w and the random variable ν. The addition of the random value causes the algorithm to "experiment" by occasionally performing actions that it would not otherwise have taken. The state component w is incremented by a value with three terms. The first term, α, is a parameter that represents the learning rate. The next term, $r - p$, represents the difference between the actual reinforcement received and the predicted reinforcement, p. This serves to normalize the reinforcement values: the absolute value of the reinforcement signal is not as important as its value relative to the average reinforcement that the agent has been receiving. The third term in the update function for w is $a - 1/2$; it has constant absolute value and the sign is used to encode which action was taken. The predicted reinforcement, p, is a weighted running average of the reinforcement values that have been received.

Sutton showed that a slightly different version of the RC algorithm is *absolutely expedient*, that is, that the expected reinforcement of individual actions taken by the algorithm is monotonically increasing over time. There are no results concerning the regret of this class of algorithms, however.

3.4 *Associative Methods*

The algorithms presented so far have addressed the case of reinforcement learning in environments that present only reinforcement values as input to the agent. A more general setting of the problem, called *associative reinforcement learning*, requires the agent to learn the best action for each of a possibly large number of input states. This

section will describe three general approaches for converting simple reinforcement-learning algorithms to work in associative environments. The first is a simple copying strategy, and the second two are
instances of a large class of associative reinforcement-learning methods developed by researchers working in the connectionist learning
paradigm. Other approaches not described here include those of Minsky [61] and Widrow, Gupta, and Maitra [104]. Barto [10] gives a good
overview of connectionist learning for control, including learning from
reinforcement.

3.4.1 Copying

The simplest method for constructing an associative reinforcement-
learner, shown in algorithm 7, consists of making a copy of the state of
the nonassociative version of the algorithm for each possible input and
training each copy separately. It requires 2^M (the number of different
input states) times the storage of the original algorithm.

In addition to being very computationally complex, the copying
method does not allow for any generalization between input instances:
that is, the agent cannot take advantage of environments in which
"similar" situations require "similar" responses.

3.4.2 Linear Associators

Sutton [89] gives methods for converting standard reinforcement-
learning algorithms to work in an associative setting in a way that
allows an agent to learn efficiently and to generalize across input states. He uses a version of the Widrow-Hoff or Adaline [105]
weight-update algorithm to associate different internal state values
with different input situations. This approach is illustrated by the
LARC (linear-associator reinforcement-comparison) algorithm shown
in algorithm 8. It is an extension of the RC algorithm to work in
environments with multiple input states.

The inputs to the algorithm are represented as $M + 1$-dimensional
vectors.[3] The output, $e(s, i)$, has value 1 or 0 depending on the dot
product of the weight vector $\mathbf{w}$ and the input i and on the value of
the random variable ν. The updating of the vector $\mathbf{w}$ is somewhat
complicated: each component is incremented by a value with four
terms. The first term, α, is a constant that represents the learning rate.
The next term, $r - p$, represents the difference between the actual reinforcement received and the predicted reinforcement, p. The predicted
reinforcement, p, is generated using a standard linear associator that

---

[3]The extra constant input allows the discrimination hyperplane learned by the algorithm
to be displaced from the origin of the space.

Let (s_0, u, e) be a learning behavior that has only reinforcement as input. We can construct a new learning behavior (s_0', u', e') with 2^M inputs as follows:

$$s_0' = array\ [1..2^M]\ of\ s_0$$
$$u'(s', i, a, r) = u(s'[i], a, r)$$
$$e'(s', i) = e(s'[i])$$

Algorithm 7
Constructing an associative algorithm by making copies of a nonassociative algorithm (COPY)

The input is represented as an $M + 1$-dimensional vector i, in which the last component is set to a constant value. The internal state, s_0, consists of two $M + 1$-dimensional vectors, $\mathbf{v}$ and $\mathbf{w}$.

$u(s, i, a, r) =$ let $p := \mathbf{v} \cdot i$
for $j = 1$ to $M + 1$ do begin
      $w_j := w_j + \alpha(r - p)(a - 1/2)i_j$
      $v_j := v_j + \beta(r - p)i_j$
end

$e(s, i) = \begin{cases} 1 & \text{if } \mathbf{w} \cdot i + \nu > 0 \\ 0 & \text{otherwise} \end{cases}$

where $\alpha > 0, 0 < \beta < 1$, and ν is a normally distributed random variable of mean 0 and standard deviation δ_y.

Algorithm 8
The linear-associator reinforcement-comparison (LARC) algorithm

learns to associate input vectors with reinforcement values by setting the weights in vector $\mathbf{v}$. The third term in the update function for $\mathbf{w}$ is $a - 1/2$: it has constant absolute value and the sign is used to encode which action was taken. The final term is i_j, which causes the jth component of the weight vector to be adjusted in proportion to the jth value of the input.

Another instance of the linear-associator approach is Barto and Anandan's *associative reward-penalty* (A_{RP}) algorithm [8]. It is a hybrid of the linear reward-penalty and linear-associator methods and was shown (under a number of restrictions, including the restriction that the set of input vectors be linearly independent) to be ϵ-optimal.

The linear-associator approach can be applied to any of the learning algorithms whose internal state consists of one or a small number of independently interpretable values for each input. If the input set is encoded by bit strings, the linear-associator approach can achieve an exponential improvement in space over the copy approach, because the size of the state of the linear-associator is proportional to the number of input bits rather than to the number of inputs. This algorithm works well on simple problems, but algorithms of this type are incapable of learning functions that are not linearly separable [62].

3.4.3 Error Backpropagation

To remedy the limitations of the linear-associator approach, multilayer connectionist learning methods have been adapted to reinforcement learning. Anderson [4], Werbos [99], and Munro [68], among others, have used error backpropagation methods[4] with hidden units in order to allow reinforcement-learning systems to learn more complex action mappings. Williams [108] presents an analysis of the use of backpropagation in associative reinforcement-learning systems. He shows that a class of reinforcement-learning algorithms that use backpropagation (an instance of which is given below) perform gradient ascent search in the direction of maximal expected reinforcement. This technique is effective and allows considerably more generalization across input states, but it requires many more presentations of the data in order for the internal units to converge to the features that they need to detect in order to compute the overall function correctly. Barto and Jordan [11] demonstrate the use of a multilayer version of the associative reward-penalty algorithm to learn nonlinear functions. This method is argued to be more biologically plausible than backpropagation, but requires considerably more presentations of the data.

As an example of the application of error backpropagation methods to reinforcement learning, Anderson's method [4] will be examined in more detail. It uses two networks: one for learning to predict reinforcement and one for learning which action to take. The weights in the action network are updated in proportion to the difference between actual and predicted reinforcement, making this an instance of the reinforcement-comparison method (discussed in section 3.3 above). Each of the networks has two layers, with all of the hidden units connected to all of the inputs and all of the inputs and hidden units connected to the outputs. The system was designed to work in worlds

---

[4]A good description of error backpropagation for supervised learning is given by Rumelhart, Hinton, and Williams [75].

with delayed reinforcement (which are discussed at greater length in chapter 8), but it is easily simplified to work in domains with instantaneous reward.

The BPRC algorithm, which is analogous to the LARC algorithm, is shown in algorithm 9 and is explained in more detail by Anderson [4]. The presentation here is simplified in a number of respects, however. In this version, there is no use of momentum and the term $(a - 1/2)$ is used to indicate the choice of action rather than the more complex expression used by Anderson. Also, Anderson uses a different distribution for the random variable ν.

The input is represented as an $M + 1$-dimensional vector i, in which the last element contains a constant value. The internal state, s_0, consists of

W_{EH} :   Weights of the hidden units in the evaluation network, an H by $M + 1$ element array initialized to small random values.

W_{EO} :   Weights of the output unit in the evaluation network, an $H + M + 1$ element array initialized to small random values.

W_{AH} :   Weights of the hidden units in the action network, an H by $M + 1$ element array initialized to small random values.

W_{AO} :   Weights of the output unit in the action network, an $H + M + 1$ element array initialized to small random values.

In addition, the algorithm makes use of the following local variables

O_{EH} :   Outputs of the hidden units in the evaluation network, an H element array.

O_{AH} :   Outputs of the hidden units in the action network, an H element array.

p :   Output of the output unit in the evaluation network.

This method is theoretically able to learn very complex functions, but tends to require many training instances before it converges. The time and space complexity for this algorithm is $O(MH)$, where M is the number of input bits and H is the number of hidden units. Also, this method is somewhat less robust than the more standard version of error backpropagation that learns from input-output pairs, because the error signal generated by the reinforcement-learning system is not always correct. In addition, the two networks must converge simultaneously to the appropriate solutions; if the learning rates are not set appropriately, the system can converge to a state in which the evaluation network decides that all input states will have a very poor expected performance, which is in fact true, given the current state of the action network. In such a situation, the weights will not be updated and the system becomes stuck.

$u(s, i, a, r) =$ {Calculate outputs of evaluation hidden units}
for $j = 1$ to H do
$\quad O_{EH}[j] := f(i \cdot W_{EH}[j])$
{Calculate result of evaluation network}
$p := W_{EO} \cdot concat(i, O_{EH})$
{Update weights of the evaluation output unit}
for $j = 1$ to $M + 1$ do
$\quad W_{EO}[j] := W_{EO}[j] + \beta\,(r - p)\,i[j]$
for $j = 1$ to H do
$\quad W_{EO}[j + M + 1] := W_{EO}[j + M + 1]$
$\qquad\qquad\qquad + \beta\,(r - p)\,O_{EH}[j]$
{Update weights of the evaluation hidden units}
for $j = 1$ to H do begin
$\quad d := (r - p)$
$\qquad sign(W_{EO}[j + M + 1])\,O_{EH}[j]\,(1 - O_{EH}[j])$
$\quad$ for $k = 1$ to $M + 1$ do
$\qquad W_{EH}[j, k] := W_{EH}[j, k] + \beta_h\,d\,i[k]$
end

{Calculate outputs of action hidden units}
for $j = 1$ to H do
$\quad O_{AH}[j] := f(i \cdot W_{AH}[j])$
{Update weights of the action output unit}
for $j = 1$ to $M + 1$ do
$\quad W_{AO}[j] := W_{AO}[j] + \rho\,(r - p)\,(a - 1/2)\,i[j]$
for $j = 1$ to H do
$\quad W_{AO}[j + M + 1] := W_{AO}[j + M + 1]$
$\qquad\qquad\qquad + \rho\,(r - p)\,(a - 1/2)\,O_{AH}[j]$
{Update weights of the action hidden units}
for $j = 1$ to H do begin
$\quad d := (r - p)\,(a - 1/2)$
$\qquad sign(W_{AO}[j + M + 1])\,O_{AH}[j]\,(1 - O_{AH}[j])$
$\quad$ for $k = 1$ to $M + 1$ do
$\qquad W_{AH}[j, k] := W_{AH}[j, k] + \rho_h\,d\,i[k]$
end

$e(s, i) =$ {Calculate outputs of action hidden units}
for $j = 1$ to H do
$\quad O_{AH}[j] := f(i \cdot W_{AH}[j])$
$$\begin{cases} 1 & \text{if } (W_{AO} \cdot concat(i, O_{AH})) + \nu > 0 \\ 0 & \text{otherwise} \end{cases}$$

where $\beta, \beta_h, \rho, \rho_h > 0$, $f(x) = 1/(1 + e^{-x})$, and ν is a normally distributed random variable of mean 0 and standard deviation δ_y.

Algorithm 9
The BPRC algorithm

3.5 Genetic Algorithms

Genetic algorithms constitute a considerably different approach to the design and implementation of reinforcement-learning systems. This section will briefly describe the general approach and point to some representative applications of genetic-algorithm methods to reinforcement learning. An excellent introduction to and survey of this field is given in Goldberg's book [36].

In their purest form, genetic algorithms (GAs) can be seen as a technique for solving optimization problems in which the elements of the solution space are coded as binary strings and in which there is a scalar objective function that can be used to compute the "fitness" of the solution represented by any string. The GA maintains a "population" of strings, which are initially chosen randomly. The fitness of each member of the population is calculated. Those with low fitness values are eliminated and members with high fitness values are reproduced in order to keep the population at a constant size. After the reproduction phase, operators are applied to introduce variation in the population. Common operators are crossover and mutation. In crossover, two population elements are chosen, at random, as operands. They are recombined by randomly choosing an index into the string and making two new strings, one that consists of the first part of the first string and the second part of the second string and one that consists of the first part of the second string and the second part of the first string. Mutation simply changes bits in population elements, with very low probability.

A more complex type of GA is the *classifier system* [40]. Developed by Holland, it consists of a population of production rules, which are encoded as strings. The rules can be executed to implement an action function that maps external inputs to external actions. When the rules chain forward to cause an external action, a reinforcement value is received from the world. Holland developed a method, called the Bucket Brigade, for propagating reinforcement back along the chain of production rules that caused the action. This method is an instance of the class of temporal difference methods, which will be discussed further in chapter 8. As a set of rules is run, each rule comes to have a relatively stable value which is used as its fitness. The standard genetic operations of reproduction, crossover, mutation, etc., are used to generate new populations of rules from old ones.

Although classifier systems are reinforcement-learners, they are not well suited for use in embedded systems. As with most production systems, there is no bound on the number of rule-firings that will be required to generate an output in response to an input, preventing the algorithm's operation from being real-time.

Grefenstette [37] has applied GA methods directly to the time-constrained problem of learning action strategies from reinforcement. The elements of the population of his system are symbolic representations of action maps. The fitness of an element is determined by executing it in the world for a number of ticks and measuring the average reinforcement. Action maps that perform well are reproduced and recombined to generate new action maps.

The GA approach works well on problems that can be effectively coded as syntactic objects in which the interpretation of individual elements is relatively context-independent and for which there are useful recombination operators. It is not yet clear what classes of problems can be so specified.

3.6 Extensions to the Model

The algorithms of the previous sections have been presented in their simplest possible forms, with only Boolean reinforcement as input and with two possible actions. It is a relatively simple matter to extend all of the algorithms except RC, LARC, and BPRC to the case of multiple actions. Because the details differ for each one, however, they shall be omitted from this discussion. The algorithms that choose an action by comparing an internal value plus noise to a threshold are more difficult to generalize in this way.

The rest of this section will briefly detail extensions of these algorithms to work in domains with non-Boolean and nonstationary reinforcement.

3.6.1 Non-Boolean Reinforcement

Algorithms BANDIT and TSETLIN have no obvious extensions to the case of non-Boolean reinforcement.

The learning-automata community considers three models of reinforcement: P, Q, and S. The P-model of reinforcement is the Boolean-reinforcement model we have already explored. In the Q-model, reinforcement is one of a finite number of possible values that are known ahead of time. These reinforcement values can always be scaled into values in the interval $[0, 1]$. Finally, the S-model allows real-valued reinforcement in the interval $[0, 1]$. The notions of expediency and optimality can be extended to apply to the Q- and S-models.

Algorithms designed for P-model environments, such as the L_{RP} and L_{RI} algorithms, can be adjusted to work in Q- and S-models as follows.

Let $\Delta_{i,0}$ be the change made to action-probability i when reinforcement 0 is received and let $\Delta_{i,1}$ be the change made when reinforcement value 1 is received. We can define, for the new models, $\Delta_{i,r}$, the change made when reinforcement value r is received as

$$\Delta_{i,r} = r\Delta_{i,1} + (1 - r)\Delta_{i,0} \; ,$$

a simple linear combination of the updates for the Boolean reinforcement cases [69].

Algorithm TS was designed to work in an S-model of reinforcement and can be used in such environments without change. Algorithm RC, as well as the associative reinforcement-comparison algorithms LARC and BPRC, work in the more general case of real-valued reinforcement that is not necessarily scaled to fall in the interval $[0, 1]$.

3.6.2 Nonstationary Environments

A world is *nonstationary* if $er(i, a)$ (the expected reinforcement of performing action a in input situation i) varies over time. It is very difficult to prove formal results about the performance of learning algorithms in nonstationary environments, but several observations can be made about which algorithms are likely to perform better in such environments. For instance, algorithms with absorbing states, such as BANDIT and L_{RI}, are inappropriate for nonstationary environments: if the world changes after the algorithm has converged, the algorithm will never sample the other actions and adjust its behavior to the changed environment. On the other hand, such algorithms as TSETLIN, L_{RP}, and RC, which continue to sample all of the actions with nonzero probability, will adapt to changes in the environment.

3.7 Conclusions

A number of effective reinforcement-learning algorithms have been developed by different research communities. The work in this volume seeks to extend and improve upon the previous work by developing more effective learning methods and by finding approaches to associative reinforcement learning that are capable of learning a broader class of functions than the linear approaches can, but doing so more space-efficiently than the copy method and with fewer input instances than are required by the error backpropagation method.

Chapter 4
Interval Estimation Method

The interval estimation method is a simple statistical algorithm for reinforcement learning that logically extends the statistical algorithms of the previous chapter. By allowing the state of the algorithm to encode not only estimates of the relative merits of the various actions, but also the degree of confidence that we have in those estimates, the interval estimation method makes it easier to control the tradeoff between acting to gain information and acting to gain reinforcement. The interval estimation algorithm performs well a variety of tasks and its basis in standard statistical methods makes its operation intuitively clear.

This chapter presents the algorithm, together with an estimate of its expected error and experimental comparisons with many of the algorithms of chapter 3; it also explores ways of extending the basic algorithm to deal with the more general learning models presented in section 3.6.

4.1 Description of the Algorithm

The interval estimation algorithm is based on the idea of storing an estimate of the expected reinforcement for each action *and* some information about how good that estimate is. The standard statistical technique of constructing confidence-interval estimates of quantities provides us with a method for doing this. The size of the confidence interval is a measure of the lack of information about the quantity being estimated. The interval estimation method can be applied in a wide variety of environments; the simplest form will be presented first, and extensions to the basic algorithm will be described in section 4.5.

The basic interval estimation algorithm is specified in algorithm 10. The state consists of simple statistics: for each action a, n_a and x_a are the number of times that the action has been executed and the number of those times that have resulted in reinforcement value 1, respectively. The evaluation function uses these statistics to compute, for each action, a confidence interval on the underlying probability,

p_a, of receiving reinforcement value 1 given that action a is executed. If n is the number of trials and x the number of successes arising from a series of Bernoulli trials with probability p, the upper bound of a $100(1 - \alpha)\%$ confidence interval for p can be approximated by $ub(x, n)$. [1] The evaluation function chooses the action with the highest upper bound on expected reinforcement.

Initially, each of the actions will have an upper bound of 1, and action 0 will be chosen arbitrarily. As more trials take place, the bounds will tighten. The interval estimation method balances acting to gain information with acting to gain reinforcement by taking advantage of the fact that there are two reasons that the upper bound for an action might be high: because there is little information about that action, causing the confidence interval to be large, or because there is information that the action is good, causing the whole confidence

---

The initial state, s_0, consists of the integer variables x_0, n_0, x_1, and n_1, each initialized to 0.

$u(s, a, r) =$ if $a = 0$ then begin

        $x_0 := x_0 + r$

        $n_0 := n_0 + 1$

    end else begin

        $x_1 := x_1 + r$

        $n_1 := n_1 + 1$

    end

$e(s) =$ if $ub(x_0, n_0) > ub(x_1, n_1)$ then

        return 0

    else

        return 1

where

$$ub(x, n) = \frac{\frac{x}{n} + \frac{z_{\alpha/2}^2}{2n} + \frac{z_{\alpha/2}}{\sqrt{n}} \sqrt{\left(\frac{x}{n}\right)\left(1 - \frac{x}{n}\right) + \frac{z_{\alpha/2}^2}{4n}}}{1 + \frac{z_{\alpha/2}^2}{n}}$$

and $z_{\alpha/2} > 0$.

Algorithm 10

The interval-estimation (IE) algorithm

[1] This is a somewhat more complex form than usual, designed to give good results for small values of n [48].

interval to be high. The parameter $z_{\alpha/2}$ is the value that will be exceeded by the value of a standard normal variable with probability $\alpha/2$. It controls the size of the confidence intervals and, thus, the relative weights given to acting to gain information and acting to gain reinforcement. As α increases, more instances of reinforcement value 0 are required to drive down the upper bound of the confidence intervals, causing more weight to be placed on acting to gain information. By the DeMoivre-Laplace theorem [48], these bounds will converge, in the limit, to the true underlying probability values, and, hence, if each action is continually attempted, this algorithm will converge to a function that satisfies Opt.

This algorithm is very closely related to, but was developed independently of, Lai's algorithm [47]. Both methods use the notion of choosing the action with the highest upper confidence bound. The confidence bounds used in Lai's algorithm are more complex than the standard statistical methods used in the interval estimation algorithm. Lai's algorithm can be shown to be optimal, but is not always computationally tractable. As we will see in section 4.4, the performance of the two algorithms is not significantly different.

In order to provide intuition about the workings of the interval-estimation algorithm, figures 12 and 13 show output from two sample runs in a simulated environment in which the actions a_0 and a_1 succeed with probabilities p_0 and p_1. The listings show the number of successes and trials of a_0 (the columns headed a0s and a0t), the upper bound on the confidence interval of p_0 (the column headed a0b) and the same for a_1 and p_1 (columns headed a1s, a1t, and a1b). These statistics are just shown at interesting points during the run of the algorithm. In figure 12, the first few trials of a_1 fail, causing the estimate of p_1 to be quite low; it will be executed a few more times, once the upper bound for p_0 is driven near .56. The run shown in figure 13 is somewhat more characteristic. The two actions have similar probabilities of success, so it takes a long time for one to establish dominance.

a0s	a0t	a0b	a1s	a1t	a1b
(14 /	19)	.88194	(0 /	1)	.79346
(81 /	138)	.66567	(0 /	2)	.65763
(85 /	147)	.65507	(0 /	3)	.56151

Figure 12
A sample run of IE with $p_0 = .55$, $p_1 = .45$, and $z_{\alpha/2} = 1.96$. In this case, it converges very quickly.

a0s	a0t	a0b	a1s	a1t	a1b
(4 /	7)	.84178	(1 /	3)	.79235
(39 /	75)	.62931	(22 /	45)	.62996
(226 /	394)	.62150	(22 /	46)	.61863
(358 /	631)	.60549	(31 /	59)	.64734
(963 /	1789)	.56128	(52 /	111)	.56080
(5548 /	9888)	.57084	(52 /	112)	.55630

Figure 13

Another sample run of IE with $p_0 = .55$, $p_1 = .45$, and $z_{\alpha/2} = 1.96$. This time, the two actions battle for a long time, but a_0 is clearly winning after 10,000 trials.

4.2 Analysis

In order to analytically compare this algorithm with other algorithms, we would like to know the regret or expected error of executing this algorithm in an environment specified by the action-success probabilities p_0 and p_1. This section informally derives an approximate expression for the regret in terms of p_0, p_1, and $z_{\alpha/2}$.

4.2.1 Regular Error

For concreteness, let us assume that $p_0 > p_1$. An error occurs every time a_1 is executed, and we expect it to be executed a number of times that is sufficient to drive the upper bound of p_1 below the actual value of p_0. We can compute this expected number of errors by setting the expected value of the upper bound on p_1 equal to p_0 and solving for n_1. The expected value of the upper bound on p_1 is approximately[2] the upper bound with the number of successes set to $n_1 p_1$. This allows us to solve the equation $ub(n_1 p_1, n_1) = p_0$ for n_1, yielding

$$n_1 = \frac{z_{\alpha/2}^2 p_0 (1 - p_0)}{(p_0 - p_1)^2} .$$

As p_0 and p_1 grow close, n_1 goes to infinity. This is as it should be — it becomes infinitely hard to tell which of the two actions is better. We can simplify this expression further by abstracting away from the actual values of p_0 and p_1 and considering their difference, δ, instead. For probabilities with a fixed difference, n_1 is maximized by setting p_0 to $1/2$ and p_1 to $1/2 + \delta$. Making this simplification, we can bound n_1 above by

---

[2]This is only an approximation because n_1 occurs inside a square-root, which does not commute with the expectation operator.

$$\frac{z^2}{4\delta^2} \; .$$

This is an approximate upper bound on the expected number of errors that will be made on a run of infinite length. The regret, or expected *amount* of error, can be obtained simply by multiplying by δ, the magnitude of the error, yielding

$$\frac{z^2}{4\delta} \; .$$

This result is somewhat disturbing, because the amount of error on an infinitely long run can be made arbitrarily large by making δ arbitrarily small. However, it is possible to bound the amount of error on a finite run of length m. The maximum expected number of errors that could be made on such a run is $m/2$ (when the two probabilities are equal, we expect to perform the actions equal numbers of times). The number of errors is monotonically decreasing in δ, so we can easily find the largest value of δ that could cause this many errors by solving the equation

$$\frac{m}{2} = \frac{z^2}{4\delta^2}$$

for δ, getting $\frac{z}{\sqrt{2m}}$. Thus, the maximum expected regular error on a run of length m would be

$$\frac{z\sqrt{m}}{2\sqrt{2}} \; ,$$

obtained by multiplying the maximum number of errors, $m/2$, by the maximum magnitude of the error. This maximum regular error is $O(m^{1/2})$, which means that the interval estimation algorithm, like the BANDIT algorithm, performs within a constant factor of optimal when the environment is as hostile as possible.

4.2.2 Error Due to Sticking
The analysis of the previous section was all carried out under the assumption that the action a_0 would be executed an infinite number of times during an infinite run. Unfortunately, this is not always the case—it is possible for a_0 to get *stuck* below a_1 in the following way. If there is a statistically unlikely series of trials of a_0 that cause the upper bound on p_0 to go *below* the actual value of p_1, then it is very likely that a_0 will never be executed again. When this happens, we shall say that a_0 is stuck. A consequence of a_0 being stuck is that errors will be made

for the remainder of the run. The process of sticking is illustrated by two sample runs. In figure 14, there is an early series of failures for a_0, causing a_1 to be dominant. However, because the upper bound on p_0 was not driven *below* p_1, the upper bound on p_1 eventually goes down far enough to cause more trials of a_0, which bring its upper bound back up. The run shown in figure 15 is a case of permanent sticking. After 0 successes in 5 trials, the upper bound on the confidence interval for p_0 is less than p_1, causing a_1 to be executed for the remainder of the run.

By assuming that once a_0 becomes stuck below a_1 it will never become unstuck, we can bound expected error due to sticking on a run in which a_0 would be executed T times, if unstuck, by

$$\sum_{t=1}^{T} sp(t)(T - t)(p_0 - p_1) \ ,$$

where the *sticking probability* $sp(t) = \Pr(ub(x_0, t) < p_1$ first becomes true at time t). It is the sum, over all time steps t on which a_0 is executed, of the probability that a_0 first gets stuck at time t times the number of time steps that remain, $(T - t)$, times the magnitude of the error, $(p_0 - p_1)$.

a0s	a0t	a0b	a1s	a1t	a1b
(0 /	2)	.65763	(4 /	8)	.78479
(0 /	3)	.56151	(67 /	137)	.57191
(1 /	4)	.69936	(70 /	146)	.55997
(16 /	34)	.63264	(78 /	176)	.51701

Figure 14
A sample run of IE with $p_0 = .55$, $p_1 = .45$, and $z_{\alpha/2} = 1.96$. The first action almost gets stuck.

a0s	a0t	a0b	a1s	a1t	a1b
(0 /	2)	.65763	(0 /	1)	.79346
(0 /	3)	.56151	(11 /	24)	.64925
(0 /	4)	.48990	(57 /	121)	.55953
(0 /	5)	.43449	(108 /	253)	.48847
(0 /	5)	.43449	(132 /	300)	.49658

Figure 15
A sample runof IE with $p_0 = .55$, $p_1 = .45$, and $z_{\alpha/2} = 1.96$. Here, the first action really does get stuck below the second.

By solving for x_0, we can transform the constraint that $ub(x_0, t) < p_1$ into

$$x_0 < tp_1 - z_{\alpha/2}\sqrt{tp_1(1 - p_1)} \ .$$

Using the theory of random walks, the probability that x_0 first goes below $tp_1 - z\sqrt{tp_1(1 - p_1)}$ at time t can be approximated by [43]

$$sp(t) = \left(1 - \frac{k}{t(p_1 - \frac{1}{2}z_{\alpha/2}\sqrt{p_1(1 - p_1)}/t)}\right)\binom{t}{k}p_0^k(1 - p_0)^{t-k} \ ,$$

where $k = \lfloor tp_1 - z_{\alpha/2}\sqrt{tp_1(1 - p_1)}\rfloor$.

4.2.3 Total Regret

An approximate upper bound on the total regret on a run of length T can finally be expressed as the sum of the regular and sticking errors:

$$\frac{z_{\alpha/2}^2}{4(p_0 - p_1)} + \sum_{t=1}^{T} sp(t)(N - t)(p_0 - p_1) \ .$$

The sticking error is summed to T for the upper bound, although the expected number of times a_0 will be executed is $T - \frac{z_{\alpha/2}^2}{4(p_0-p_1)}$. There has not yet been any discussion of appropriate values for $z_{\alpha/2}$ to take on. The value of $z_{\alpha/2}$ determines the size of the confidence interval and, therefore, the number of trials it takes to drive an upper bound below a certain value. Thus, regular error *increases* as $z_{\alpha/2}$ increases and the interval gets larger. But, as the size of the confidence interval increases, error due to sticking *decreases* as $z_{\alpha/2}$ increases. This trade-off is illustrated in figure 16, which plots the approximate forms for regular error and error due to sticking as functions of $z_{\alpha/2}$. If we had any *a priori* expectations about the underlying values of p_0 and p_1, we could choose $z_{\alpha/2}$ to minimize regret.

4.3 Empirical Results

The approximations of the previous section were tested by comparing predicted results against actual results of the interval estimation algorithm in a simulated world. The algorithm was executed for δ ranging, in increments of .05, from .05 to .6, with p_1 and p_2 equally spaced about .5 (for $\delta = .1$, $p_1 = .55$ and $p_2 = .45$.) For each value of δ, 1079 runs of length 10,000 were conducted. The variable $z_{\alpha/2}$ had value 1.96 throughout. Figure 17 contains a plot, for each δ, of the mean error of the runs that did not stick, together with the predicted error. The predictions seem to be fairly accurate for regular error. Figure 18 shows

error

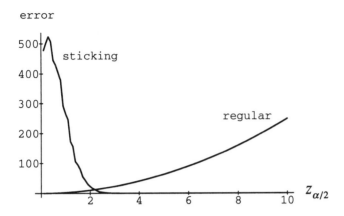

Figure 16
Expected regular error and sticking error plotted as a function of $z_{\alpha/2}$

the mean error due to sticking for each δ, along with the predicted values. This prediction is somewhat less accurate. Nonetheless, these results are encouraging, because we can see that, in these cases, the total expected error is quite small—less than 50 fewer instants of reinforcement value 1 than expected from the optimal algorithm for runs of length 10,000.

4.4 Experimental Comparisons

This section reports the results of a set of experiments designed to compare the performance of the interval estimation algorithm with the most promising existing reinforcement-learning algorithms.

4.4.1 Algorithms and Environments
The following algorithms were compared in these experiments:

- BANDIT (algorithm 1)
- L_{RP} (algorithm 3)
- L_{RI} (algorithm 4)
- TS (algorithm 5)
- RC (algorithm 6)
- LAI (described briefly in Section 3.1)
- IE (algorithm 10)

Each of the algorithms was tested in four different environments. The environments generate Boolean reinforcement, with reinforcement value 1 resulting with probability p_0 after doing action a_0 and with

regular error

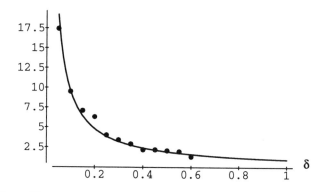

Figure 17

Regular error as a function of δ; dots indicate the mean regular error on 1079 runs of length 10,000; the curve is predicted error.

sticking error

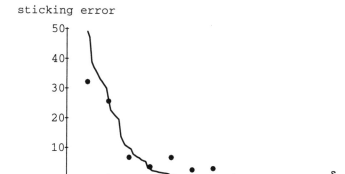

Figure 18

Error due to sticking as a function of δ; dots indicate the mean error due to sticking on 1079 runs of length 10,000; the curve is predicted error.

probability p_1 after doing action a_1. Table 1 shows the values of p_0 and p_1 for each environment.

4.4.2 Parameter Tuning

Each of the algorithms, except LAI, has a single parameter that can be chosen to make the algorithm more or less conservative;[3] the best

---

[3] Actually, RC also has parameters β and σ, but following Sutton [89], these parameters were held constant at .1 and .3, respectively.

Table 1
Parameters of test environments

Task	p_0	p_1
1	.9	.1
2	.6	.4
3	.9	.8
4	.2	.1

Table 2
Best parameter value for each algorithm in each environment

ALG-TASK	1	2	3	4
BANDIT(k)	1	12	10	10
L_{RP} (α)	.60	.60	.30	.40
L_{RI} (α)	.55	.1	.05	.15
TS (λ)	.30	.20	.20	.35
RC (α)	.40	.30	.15	.50
IE ($z_{\alpha/2}$)	3.0	2.0	3.0	2.0

choice of value for these parameters typically depends on the length of the run, because it is more important to ensure that an absorbing algorithm converges to the correct action on a long run. For each algorithm and environment, a series of 100 trials of length 1000 were run with different values of the parameter. Table 2 shows the best parameter value found for each algorithm and environment pair.

Although these experiments can be illuminating, in actual applications we will typically want to apply these algorithms to situations in which the underlying probabilities are not known or there is not enough time to make many runs with different parameter values. In such situations, an algorithm that performs well over a wide range of problems with the same parameter value is to be preferred over one that performs well when the parameter is chosen exactly appropriately for the problem, but poorly otherwise. As we can see in table 2, the interval estimation algorithm operates at its best in all of these problems with a $z_{\alpha/2}$ value between 2 and 3—this roughly corresponds to using 95% or 99% confidence intervals, values that, interestingly, are often used by human decision-makers.

4.4.3 Results
After choosing the best parameter value for each algorithm and environment, the performance of the algorithms was compared on 100 runs of length 1000. The performance metric was average reinforcement per tick, averaged over the entire run. The results are shown in table 3.

Table 3
Average reinforcement over 100 runs of length 1000

ALG-TASK	1	2	3	4
BANDIT	.8982	.5856	.8892	.1888
L_{RP}	.8172	.5190	.8665	.1521
L_{RI}	.8911	.5872	.8780	.1934
TS	.8979	.5893	.8941	.1870
RC	.8988	.5890	.8897	.1930
LAI	.8960	.5950	.8949	.1963
IE	.9004	.5953	.8937	.1972
random	.5000	.5000	.8500	.1500
optimal	.9000	.6000	.9000	.2000

These results do not tell the entire story, however. It is important to test for statistical significance to be relatively sure that the ordering of one algorithm over another did not arise by chance. Figure 19 shows, for each task, a pictorial representation of the results of a 1-sided t-test applied to each pair of experimental results. The graphs encode a partial order of significant dominance, with solid lines representing significance at the .95 level and dashed lines representing significance at the .85 level. We can see that the interval-estimation algorithm dominates in nearly every task. On Task 3 its average reinforcement value was slightly lower than that of the TS and LAI algorithms, but this difference was not significant. The LAI algorithm performs well on Tasks 2, 3, and 4, which have a relatively small separation between payoff probabilities. It does much worse on Task 1, in which the separation is large. Because the algorithm is designed to be optimal on infinite runs, it must guard against premature convergence to the wrong action. The larger the separation, the worse the consequences of choosing the wrong action, so the LAI algorithm is more conservative than the other algorithms in such cases. The L_{RP} algorithm is, as expected, uniformly suboptimal, and the rest of the algorithms perform about the same at quite a high level.

Another view of the relative performance of the algorithms is given by examining their learning curves. A learning curve is a plot of expected reinforcement values versus time, which shows the rate of performance improvement. Figures 20, 21, 22, and 23 contain, for each task, the superimposed learning curves of each algorithm for that task. Each point represents the average reinforcement received over a sequence of 50 ticks, averaged over 100 runs of length 1000. For Tasks 1 and 2, the curves are hard to differentiate; the order of the labels on the right hand sides of the graphs indicates the average relative performance of the algorithms on the first sample of 50 ticks.

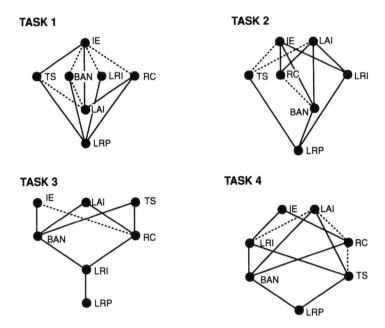

Figure 19
Significant dominance partial order among algorithms for each task

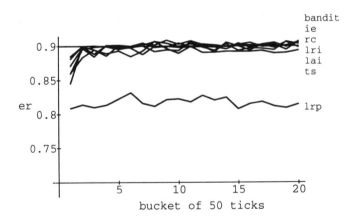

Figure 20
Learning curves for Task 1

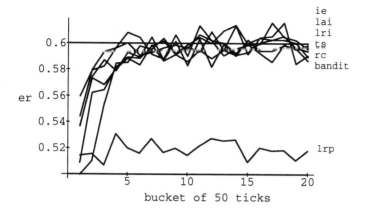

Figure 21
Learning curves for Task 2

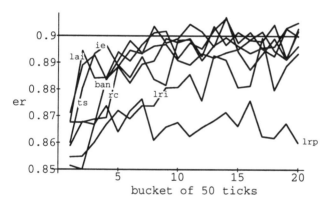

Figure 22
Learning curves for Task 3

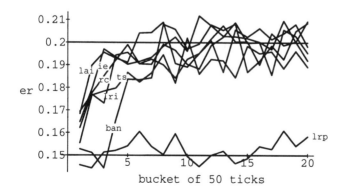

Figure 23
Learning curves for Task 4

4.5 Extensions

As with the algorithms of chapter 3, the interval estimation algorithm
can be extended to work in more complex environments. All of the
extensions described in this section have been implemented and tested
in simulated environments.

4.5.1 Multiple Inputs and Actions
The interval estimation algorithm can be directly generalized to multiple actions. Statistics are collected for each action and are used to
construct upper bounds. The action with the highest upper bound is
chosen to be executed at each tick.

There is no specific way to tailor the interval estimation algorithm to
work in situations where there are multiple input states. The method
of making a copy of the internal state for each possible input situation
can be applied to the interval estimation algorithm, but because there
is more than a single value associated with each input state, it would
be difficult to apply the linear association or error backpropagation
methods.

4.5.2 Real-valued Reinforcement
Rather than thinking of choosing the action with the highest probability of succeeding, we can think of choosing the action with the highest
expected reinforcement. Under this view, the interval estimation process can be applied to the expected value of reinforcement given that
the action a is executed in situation i. If the reinforcement for each
tick is binomially distributed with parameter p, this is exactly what is
taking place in the version of the algorithm presented in section 4.1.

Simple extensions can be made if a different probabilistic distribution underlies the reinforcement associated with taking action. In
order to handle real-valued reinforcement, for example, we can apply
one of the following methods: assuming the normal distribution and
using nonparametric statistics.

If the reinforcement values are normally distributed, we can use
standard statistical methods to construct a confidence interval for the
expected value. In order to do this, we must keep the following statistics: n, the number of trials, $\sum x$, the sum of the reinforcement received
so far, and $\sum x^2$, the sum of squares of the individual reinforcement
values. The upper bound of a $100(1 - \alpha)$ % confidence interval for the
mean of the distribution can be computed by

$$nub(n, \sum x, \sum x^2) = \bar{y} + t^{(n-1)}_{\alpha/2} \frac{s}{\sqrt{n}}$$

where $\bar{y} = x/n$ is the sample mean,

$$s = \sqrt{\frac{n \sum x^2 - (\sum x)^2}{n(n-1)}}$$

is the sample standard deviation, and $t_{\alpha/2}^{(n-1)}$ is Student's t function with $n-1$ degrees of freedom at the $\alpha/2$ confidence level [88]. Other than using a different statistical method to compute the upper bound of the expected reinforcement, the algorithm remains the same.

Even when the reinforcement values cannot be assumed to be normally distributed, the interval estimation algorithm can be implemented using simple nonparametric statistics.[4] In this case, it is not possible to derive an upper bound on expected value from summary statistics, so we must keep the individual reinforcement values. Obviously, it is impossible to store them all, so only the data in a sliding window are kept. The nonparametric version of the interval estimation algorithm requires another parameter, w, that determines the size of the window of data. The data are kept sorted by value as well as by time received. The upper bound of a $100(1-\alpha)\%$ confidence interval for the center of the underlying distribution (whatever it may be) can be calculated, using the ordinary sign test [33], to be the $(n-u)$th element of the sorted data, if they are labelled, starting at 1, from smallest to largest, where n is minimum of w and the number of instances received. The value u is chosen to be the largest value such that

$$\sum_{k=0}^{u} \binom{n}{k} .5^n \leq \alpha/2 \ .$$

For large values of n, u can be approximated using the normal distribution.

4.5.3 Nonstationary Environments
The basic version of the interval estimation algorithm can converge to absorbing states and, as noted in section 3.6.2, that makes it inappropriate for use in nonstationary environments. One way to modify the algorithm in order to fix this problem is to decay all of the statistics associated with a particular input value by some value δ less than, but

---

[4]Nonparametric methods tend to work poorly when there are a small number of discrete values with very different magnitudes. Practical results have been obtained in such cases by using methods for the normal distribution with the modification that each action is performed at least a certain fixed number of times. This prevents the sample variance from going to 0 on small samples with identical values.

typically near, 1, whenever that input value is received. This decaying will have the effect that the recorded number of trials of an action that is not being executed decreases over time, causing the confidence interval to grow, the upper bound to increase, and the neglected action to be executed again. If its underlying expected value has increased, that will be revealed when the action is executed and it may come to be the dominant action.

This technique may be similarly applied when using statistical methods for normally distributed reinforcement values. The nonparametric method described above is already partially suited to nonstationary environments because old data only has a finite period of influence (of length w) on the choices of the algorithm. It can be made more responsive to environmental changes by occasionally dropping a data point from the list of an action that is not being executed. This will cause the upper bound to increase, eventually forcing the action to be executed again.

Another method of changing an algorithm to work in nonstationary environments is to choose the "wrong action" (one that would not have been chosen by the algorithm) with some probability that varies inversely with n, the number of trials that have taken place so far. As time passes, it becomes less and less likely to do an action that is not prescribed by the current learned policy, but executing these "wrong" actions ensures that if they have become "right" due to changes in the environment, the algorithm will adapt. This method is more suited to situations in which environmental changes are expected to be more likely to happen early in a run, rather than later.

4.6 Conclusion

The interval estimation algorithm is of theoretical interest because of its simplicity and its direct ties to standard statistical methods. It performs at a consistently high level, not significantly different from LAI, which has been shown to be optimal for infinite runs, but is potentially computationally unbounded. In addition, following chapters will demonstrate that the interval estimation techniques used in IE can also be applied to other learning problems, such as learning functions in k-DNF from reinforcement and learning from delayed reinforcement.

Chapter 5

Divide and Conquer

Because we wish to reduce the complexity of learning algorithms, it is useful to think of the inputs and outputs as being encoded in some binary code. The problem, then, is one of constructing a function that maps a number of input bits to a number of output bits. If we can construct algorithms that effectively learn interesting classes of functions with time and space complexity that is polynomial in the number of input and output bits, we will have improved upon the previous group of algorithms.

Having decided to view the problem as one of learning a mapping from many input bits to many output bits, we can reduce this problem to the problem of learning a mapping from many input bits to one output bit. This chapter discusses such a problem reduction, first describing it informally, then proving its correctness. It concludes with empirical results of applying the reduction method to two moderately complex learning problems.

5.1 Boolean-Function Learners

A Boolean-function learner (BFL) is a reinforcement-learning behavior that learns a mapping from many input bits to one output bit. It has the same input-output structure as any of the algorithms discussed so far, but is limited to having only two actions. We can describe a BFL with k input bits in the general form of a learning behavior where $\hat{s}_{0,k}$ is the initial state, $\hat{u}_k$ is the update function and $\hat{e}_k$ is the evaluation function.

A BFL is *correct* if and only if whenever it chooses an action a in situation i, $er(i,a) \geq er(i,\neg a)$. That is, it always chooses the action that has the higher expected reinforcement.

5.2 Cascade Algorithm

We can construct an algorithm that learns an action map with N output bits by using N copies of a Boolean-function learning algorithm,

one dedicated to learning the function corresponding to each individual output bit. This simple scheme is called the TEAM algorithm and is
shown schematically in figure 24. It can be described as a learning behavior, defined in terms of calls on the components of the underlying
BFL, as shown in algorithm 11.

There is a large potential problem with the TEAM method: when the
collection of BFLs generates an output pattern that does not result in
a good reinforcement value, it is difficult to know whose fault it was.
Perhaps only one of the bits was "wrong." To avoid this problem,
often referred to the as "structural credit assignment" problem, we
construct a learning algorithm (shown schematically in figure 25) from
N cascaded BFLs. The BFL dedicated to learning to generate the first
output bit (referred to as BFL_0) has the M real input bits as input. The
next one, BFL_1, has the M real inputs as well as the output of BFL_0 as
input. In general, BFL_k will have $M + k$ bits of input, corresponding to
the real inputs and the outputs of the k lower-numbered BFLs. Each
one learns what its output bit should be, given the input situation and
the values of the output bits of the lower-numbered BFLs. The cascade
algorithm can be described in terms of component learning behaviors
as shown in algorithm 12.

The complexity of the CASCADE algorithm can be expressed as a
function of the complexity of the component BFLs, letting $S(\hat{s}_{0,k})$ be
the size of the initial state of a BFL with k input bits, $T(\hat{u}_k)$ be the time
for the BFL update function with k input bits, and $T(\hat{e}_k)$ be the time for
the BFL evaluation function with k input bits. For the entire CASCADE
algorithm with M input bits and N output bits, the size of the state is

$$O(\sum_{j=0}^{N-1} S(\hat{s}_{0,M+j})) \ ,$$

which reduces to

$$O(N \, S(\hat{s}_{0,M+N})) \ ;$$

the time for an update is

$$O(N \, T(\hat{u}_{M+N})) \ ;$$

and the time for an evaluation is

$$O(N \, T(\hat{e}_{M+N})) \ .$$

Given efficient algorithms for implementing the BFLs, the CASCADE
method can construct an efficient algorithm for learning functions with
any number of output bits.[1]

[1]This assumes that $S(\hat{s}_{0,k})$, $T(\hat{u}_k)$, and $T(\hat{e}_k)$ are all monotonically nondecreasing in k.

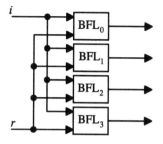

Figure 24
A TEAM of Boolean-function learners

$$s_0 = \text{array of length } N \text{ of } \hat{s}_{0,M}$$
$$u(s,i,a,r) = \text{for } j := 0 \text{ to } N-1$$
$$\hat{u}_M(s[j],i,a[j],r)$$
$$e(h,i) = \text{for } j := 0 \text{ to } N-1$$
$$a[j] := \hat{e}_M(s[j],i)$$
$$\text{return } a$$

Algorithm 11
The TEAM algorithm

This efficiency comes at a price, however. Even if there is no noise in the environment, a mistake made on bit j will cause the reinforcement information for bits 0 through $j-1$ to be in error. To see this, consider the case of two output bits. Given input instance i, bit 0 is generated to have the value 1; then, bit 1 is generated, as a function of both i and the value of bit 0, to have the value 0. If the correct response in this case was $\langle 1,1 \rangle$, then each of the bits will be given low reinforcement values, even though bit 0 was correct. This brings to light another requirement of the BFLs: they must work correctly in nonstationary environments. As the higher-numbered BFLs are in the process of converging, the lower-numbered ones will be getting reinforcement values that are not necessarily indicative of how well they are performing. Once the higher-numbered BFLs have converged, the lower-numbered BFLs must be able to disregard their earlier training and learn to act correctly given the functions that the higher-numbered BFLs are now implementing.

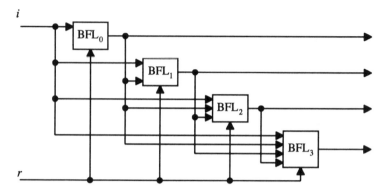

i

Figure 25
A CASCADE of Boolean-function learners

$$s_0 = \text{array of } \hat{s}_{0,M+j} \text{ where } j \text{ goes from 0 to } N-1$$
$$u(s,i,a,r) = \text{for } j := 0 \text{ to } N-1$$
$$\hat{u}_{M+j}(s[j], concat(i, a[0..j-1]), a[j], r)$$
$$e(h,i) = \text{ for } j := 0 \text{ to } N-1$$
$$a[j] := \hat{e}_{M+j}(s[j], concat(i, a[0..j-1]))$$
$$\text{return } a$$

Algorithm 12
The CASCADE algorithm

5.3 Correctness and Convergence

In order to show that the CASCADE algorithm works, we must demonstrate two points: first, that if the component BFLs converge to correct behavior then the behavior of the entire construction will be correct; second, that the component BFLs are trained in a way that guarantees that they will converge to correct behavior. These requirements will be referred to as correctness and convergence.

5.3.1 Correctness

This section presents a proof that the cascade construction is correct for the case of two output bits. Similar proofs can be constructed for cases with any number of bits. Assume that the two BFLs have already converged, the first one to the function f_0, and the second to the function f_1. The following formula asserts that the function f_0 is correct, given the choice of f_1:

$$\forall i. \; er(i, \langle f_0(i), f_1(i, f_0(i)) \rangle) \geq er(i, \langle \neg f_0(i), f_1(i, \neg f_0(i)) \rangle) \; ; \tag{1}$$

that is, that for any value of the input i, it is better for the first bit to have the value $f_0(i)$ than its opposite. Similarly, we can assert that the function f_1 is correct:

$$\forall i, b.\ er(i, \langle b, f_1(i, b) \rangle) \geq er(i, \langle b, \neg f_1(i, b) \rangle) \ ; \tag{2}$$

that is, that for any values of input i and first bit b (b is the output of f_0 in the cascade), it is better that the second bit have the value $f_1(i, b)$ than its opposite.

We would like to show that the composite output of the cascade algorithm is correct: that is, that for any input, no two-bit output has higher expected reinforcement than the one that is actually chosen by f_0 and f_1. This can be stated formally as the following conjunction:

$$\forall i.\ er(i, \langle f_0(i), f_1(i, f_0(i)) \rangle) \geq er(i, \langle \neg f_0(i), f_1(i, f_0(i)) \rangle) \ \wedge \tag{3}$$

$$\forall i.\ er(i, \langle f_0(i), f_1(i, f_0(i)) \rangle) \geq er(i, \langle f_0(i), \neg f_1(i, f_0(i)) \rangle) \ \wedge \tag{4}$$

$$\forall i.\ er(i, \langle f_0(i), f_1(i, f_0(i)) \rangle) \geq er(i, \langle \neg f_0(i), \neg f_1(i, f_0(i)) \rangle) \ . \tag{5}$$

The first conjunct, 3, can be shown with a proof by cases. In the first case, given first argument i, function f_1 is insensitive to its second argument: that is, $\forall x.\ f_1(i, x) = f_1(i, \neg x)$. In this case,

$$er(i, \langle \neg f_0(i), f_1(i, f_0(i)) \rangle) = er(i, \langle \neg f_0(i), f_1(i, \neg f_0(i)) \rangle) \ ; \tag{6}$$

from 6 and assumption 1 we can conclude that

$$er(i, \langle f_0(i), f_1(i, f_0(i)) \rangle) \geq er(i, \langle \neg f_0(i), f_1(i, f_0(i)) \rangle) \ .$$

In the second case, function f_1 is sensitive to its second argument when the first argument has value i; that is, $\forall x.\ f_1(i, x) = \neg f_1(i, \neg x)$. In this case,

$$er(i, \langle \neg f_0(i), f_1(i, f_0(i)) \rangle) = er(i, \langle \neg f_0(i), \neg f_1(i, \neg f_0(i)) \rangle) \ . \tag{7}$$

Combining assumptions 1 and 2, we can derive

$$er(i, \langle f_0(i), f_1(i, f_0(i)) \rangle) \geq er(i, \langle \neg f_0(i), \neg f_1(i, \neg f_0(i)) \rangle) \ . \tag{8}$$

From 7 and 8, we have our desired conclusion, that

$$er(i, \langle f_0(i), f_1(i, f_0(i)) \rangle) \geq er(i, \langle \neg f_0(i), f_1(i, f_0(i)) \rangle) \ .$$

The second conjunct, 4, follows directly from assumption 2.

The third conjunct, 5, also requires a proof based on cases similar those used in the proof of the first conjunct. In the first case, $\forall x.\ f_1(i, x) = f_1(i, \neg x)$, so

$$er(i, \langle \neg f_0(i), \neg f_1(i, f_0(i)) \rangle) = er(i, \langle \neg f_0(i), \neg f_1(i, \neg f_0(i)) \rangle) \ . \tag{9}$$

From 9 and result 8 above, we can derive

$$er(i, \langle f_0(i), f_1(i, f_0(i)) \rangle) \geq er(i, \langle \neg f_0(i), \neg f_1(i, f_0(i)) \rangle) \ .$$

In the second case, $\forall x.\ f_1(i, x) = \neg f_1(i, \neg x)$, so

$$er(i, \langle \neg f_0(i), \neg f_1(i, f_0(i)) \rangle) = er(i, \langle \neg f_0(i), f_1(i, \neg f_0(i)) \rangle) \ .$$

Combining this result with assumption 1, we get the desired result, that

$$er(i, \langle f_0(i), f_1(i, f_0(i)) \rangle) \geq er(i, \langle \neg f_0(i), \neg f_1(i, f_0(i)) \rangle) \ .$$

Thus, we can see that local assumptions of correctness for each BFL are sufficient to guarantee global correctness of the entire cascade algorithm.

5.3.2 Convergence

Now, we must show that the BFLs are trained in a way that justifies assumptions 1 and 2 above. It is difficult to make this argument precise without making very strong assumptions about the BFLs and the environment. Informally, the argument is as follows. The highest-numbered BFL (BFL_N) always gets correct reinforcement and so converges to the correct strategy; this is because, independent of what the lower-numbered BFLs are doing, it can learn always to make the best of a bad situation. Once this has happened, BFL_{N-1} will get correct reinforcement; because its internal learning algorithm works in non-stationary environments, it will converge to behave in the best way it can in light of what BFL_N does (which now is correct). This argument can be made all the way up to BFL_0.

In general, the convergence process may work somewhat differently. Convergence happens on an input-by-input basis, because there is no guarantee that the whole input space will be explored during any finite prefix of a run of the agent. Rather, an input comes in from the world and all the BFLs except BFL_N generate their output bits. This constitutes a learning instance for BFL_N, which can gain information about what to do in this situation. After this situation has occurred a few times, BFL_N will converge *for that input situation* (including the bits generated by the lower-numbered BFLs). As the lower-numbered BFLs begin to change their behavior, they may generate output patterns that BFL_N has never seen, requiring BFL_N to learn what to do in that situation before the lower-numbered BFLs can continue their learning process.

5.4 Empirical Results

As an illustration of the CASCADE reduction method, this section out-
lines its use, in conjunction with the interval estimation algorithm, to
solve a complex learning problem. As a baseline for comparison, we
also consider the TEAM algorithm and the use of the interval estimation
algorithm in conjunction with the method of adding extra copies of
the basic statistical algorithm to handle multiple actions. These three
methods will be compared in terms of computational complexity and
performance on the learning problem.

5.4.1 Complexity

Table 4 shows the space, update time, and evaluation time complexity
of the three algorithms for M input bits and N output bits. The space
complexity of an instance of the interval estimation algorithm with a
copy of the basic algorithm for each input-action pair is $O(2^{M+N})$. The
TEAM method requires N copies of the algorithm each with 1 output
bit and M input bits and the CASCADE method requires N copies of
the algorithm, each with 1 output bit and up to $M + N - 1$ input bits.

The time complexity of an update operation (if indexing is ignored)
is constant for the IE method; the TEAM and CASCADE methods require
each component BFL to be updated, using $O(N)$ time.

The time complexity of an evaluation using the IE method is $O(2^N)$,
because each possible action must be evaluated. Using the TEAM and
CASCADE methods, however, it is $O(N)$, because only 2 actions must
be evaluated for each output bit.

Each cycle of a learning behavior requires one update and one evaluation: for the IE method this requires $O(1) + O(2^N) = O(2^N)$ time; for
the TEAM and CASCADE methods it requires $O(N) + O(N) = O(N)$ time.
Thus, the TEAM method is the most time and space efficient; the space
complexity is somewhat greater using the CASCADE method, but computation time is still considerably shorter than for the basic IE method.

Table 4
Complexities of IE, TEAM and CASCADE methods using IE to implement the component
BFLs

	IE	TEAM	CASCADE
SPACE	$O(2^{M+N})$	$O(N2^M)$	$O(N2^{M+N})$
UPDATE TIME	$O(1)$	$O(N)$	$O(N)$
EVAL TIME	$O(2^N)$	$O(N)$	$O(N)$

Table 5
Average reinforcement over 5 runs. Runs of adder task are of length 100,000; runs of random task are of length 30,000.

ALG-TASK	ADDER	RAND
IE	.5887	.6192
TEAM + IE	.3108	.1004
CASCADE + IE	.6647	.6428
random	.1250	.1008
optimal	.9000	.9000

5.4.2 Performance

The algorithms were tested on two moderately complex reinforcement-learning problems. The first was that of learning to be an n-bit adder: the learner has $2n$ input bits, representing the addends, and n output bits, representing the result. It is considered to be correct if the output bits are the binary sum of the first n input bits and the second n input bits. For this experiment, a 5-bit adder problem was used; it has fairly high complexity, with 1024 possible inputs and 32 possible outputs. The second domain was an artificial domain chosen to demonstrate generalization in the output space. It had 3 input bits and 10 output bits; five of the output bits were randomly selected Boolean functions of the inputs and four of them were "don't cares," which did not affect the correctness of an output. In each case, if the correct output was generated, reinforcement value 1 would be received with probability .9; if the output was incorrect, reinforcement value 1 would be received with probability .1. Inputs were chosen randomly according to the uniform distribution.

Table 5 shows the results of five runs of length 100,000 of each of the algorithms in the adder environment and five runs of length 30,000 in the random environment. The α parameter of the IE algorithm had value 2.0 throughout; the instances of IE in the TEAM had decay rate of .99999 and those in the CASCADE had value .99. These parameter values were determined by informal experimentation. We can see that in each case, the CASCADE algorithm performed much better than the IE algorithm, which, in turn, performed much better than the TEAM algorithm. All of these differences are statistically significant. Figures 26 and 27 show the superimposed learning curves of the algorithms in the two domains, which plot expected reinforcement per tick against time during the run. The data points represent averages of 1000 time steps (300 time steps for the random domain), themselves averaged over the five runs.

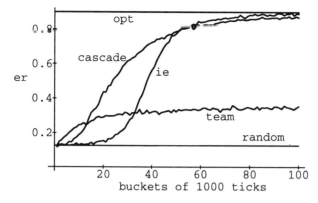

Figure 26
Learning curves for the 5-bit adder domain

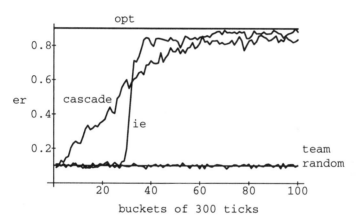

Figure 27
Learning curves for the 3-10 bit random domain

Examination of the learning curves reveals the nature of the performance differences between the algorithms. The first thing to notice is the very poor asymptotic performance of the TEAM algorithm. Because the output bits are generated completely independently, the algorithm is unable to explore the output space in any sort of systematic way, so it converges too soon on suboptimal solutions. The CASCADE algorithm avoids this problem by conditioning the output bits on one another, which allows it to make the necessary individual action choices to explore the entire space. Another important feature of these curves is the initial learning rates: TEAM learns the fastest, followed by CAS-CADE and then IE. The reason for this is that, in the TEAM and CASCADE methods, the output bits are being trained in parallel and the agent will not, in general, have to try all (or even half) of the 2^N possible actions in each input situation before finding the correct one. The input spaces for TEAM are even smaller than those for CASCADE. The last thing to notice is that the asymptotic performance of CASCADE is not quite optimal; this is due to the fact that the decay rate must be set to some value less than 1 in order for the BFLs to overcome their initially poor reinforcement. This problem could be easily fixed by moving the decay rate toward 1 as a function of time.

At first, it may seem that the algorithm is somehow taking advantage of the structure of the adder problem, because the general solution to the n-bit adder problem involves feeding intermediate results (carries) to later parts of the computation. Upon closer examination, however, it is clear that the intermediate results are simply less-significant output bits, which are not related to the values of the carries and do not simplify the computation of the more-significant output bits. Thus, the performance of the CASCADE algorithm cannot be attributed to the special structure of the adder problem.

5.5 Conclusion

The CASCADE method provides an effective way to combine a collection of Boolean-function learning components into a learner with a large output space. It gives both a reduction in run-time complexity and an improvement in on-line performance at the cost of a slight increase in space. In addition, it allows us to focus on the simpler problem of learning Boolean functions, knowing that solutions to that problem can be combined effectively into solutions for the more general problem.

Chapter 6

Learning Boolean Functions in k-DNF

6.1 Background

Algorithms, like the interval estimation algorithm, that simply make a copy of their state for each input instance require space proportional to the number of inputs in the space; as we begin to apply such algorithms to real-world problems, their time and space requirements will make them impractical. In addition, such algorithms completely compartmentalize the information they have about individual input situations. If such an algorithm learns to perform a particular action in one input situation, that knowledge has no influence on what it will do in similar input situations. In realistic environments, an agent cannot expect ever to encounter all of the input situations, let alone have enough experience with each one to learn the appropriate response. Thus, it is important to develop algorithms that will generalize across input situations.

It is important to note, however, that in order to find more efficient algorithms, we must give up something. What we will be giving up is the possibility of learning any arbitrary action mapping. In the worst case, the only way to represent a mapping is as a complete look-up table, which is what the multiple-input version of the interval estimation algorithm does. There are many useful and interesting functions that can be represented much more efficiently, and the remainder of this work will rest on the hope and expectation that an agent can learn to act effectively in interesting environments without needing action maps of pathological complexity.

In the previous chapter, we saw that the problem of learning an action map with many output bits can be reduced to the problem of learning a collection of action maps with single Boolean outputs. Such action maps can be described by formulae in propositional logic, in which the atoms are input bits. The formula $(i_1 \wedge i_2) \vee \neg i_0$ describes an action map that performs action 1 whenever input bits 1 and 2 are on or input bit 0 is off and performs action 0 otherwise. When there are only two possible actions, we can describe the class of action maps that are learnable by an algorithm in terms of syntactic restrictions on the corresponding class of propositional formulae. This method is widely used in the literature on computational learning theory.

A restriction that has proved useful to the concept-learning community is to the class of functions that can be expressed as propositional formulae in k-DNF. A formula is said to be in *disjunctive normal form* (DNF) if it is syntactically organized into a disjunction of purely conjunctive terms; there is a simple algorithmic method for converting any formula into DNF [28]. A formula is in the class k-DNF if and only if its representation in DNF contains only conjunctive terms of length k or less. There is no restriction on the number of conjunctive terms—just their length. Whenever k is less than the number of atoms in the domain, the class k-DNF is a restriction on the class of functions.

The next section presents Valiant's algorithm for learning functions in k-DNF from input-output pairs. The following sections describe algorithms for learning action maps in k-DNF from reinforcement and present the results of an empirical comparison of their performance. For each reinforcement-learning algorithm, the inputs are bit-vectors of length M, plus a distinguished reinforcement bit; the outputs are single bits.

6.2 Learning k-DNF from Input-Output Pairs

Valiant was one of the first to consider the restriction to learning functions expressible in k-DNF [95, 96]. He developed an algorithm, shown in algorithm 13, for learning functions in k-DNF from input-output pairs, which actually only uses the input-output pairs with output 0.[1]

The VALIANT algorithm returns the set of terms remaining in T, with the interpretation that their disjunction is the concept that was learned by the algorithm. This method simply examines a fixed number of negative instances and removes any term from T that would have caused one of the negative instances to be satisfied.[2]

6.3 Combining the LARC and VALIANT Algorithms

Given our interest in restricted classes of functions, we can construct a hybrid algorithm for learning action maps in k-DNF. It hinges on

---

[1]The choice of L is not relevant to our reinforcement-learning scenario—the details are described in Valiant's papers [95, 96].

[2]Valiant's presentation of the algorithm defines T to be the set of conjunctive terms of length k *or less* over the set of atoms and their negations; however, because any term of length less than k can be represented as a disjunction of terms of length k, we use a smaller set T for simplicity in exposition and slightly more efficient computation time.

Let T be initialized to the set of conjunctive terms of length k over the set of atoms (corresponding to the input bits) and their negations, and let L be the number of learning instances required to learn the concept to the desired accuracy.

```
for i := 1 to L do begin
        v := randomly drawn negative instance
        T := T− any term that is satisfied by v
end
return T
```

Algorithm 13
Valiant's algorithm for learning functions in k-DNF from input-output pairs

the simple observation that any such function is a linear combination of terms in the set T, where T is the set of conjunctive terms of length k over the set of atoms (corresponding to the input bits) and their negations. It is possible to take the original M-bit input signal and transduce it to a wider signal that is the result of evaluating each member of T on the original inputs. We can use this new signal as input to a linear-associative reinforcement learning algorithm, such as Sutton's LARC algorithm (algorithm 8). If there are M input bits, the set T has size $\binom{2M}{k}$ because we are choosing from the set of input bits and their negations. However, we can eliminate all elements that contain both an atom and its negation, yielding a set of size $2^k\binom{M}{k}$. The combined algorithm, called LARCKDNF, is described formally in algorithm 14 and schematically in figure 28.

The space required by the LARCKDNF algorithm, as well as the time to update the internal state or to evaluate an input instance, is proportional to the size of T, and thus, $O(M^k)$.

6.4 Interval Estimation Algorithm for k-DNF

The interval estimation algorithm for k-DNF is, like the LARCKDNF algorithm, based on Valiant's algorithm, but it uses standard statistical estimation methods, like those used in the IE algorithm, rather than weight adjustments.

The algorithm will first be described independent of particular statistical tests, which will be introduced later in this section. We shall need the following definitions, however. An input bit vector *satisfies* a term whenever all the bits mentioned positively in the term have value 1 in the input and all the bits mentioned negatively in the term have value 0 in the input. The quantity $er(t, a)$ is the expected value

Let F_T be a function mapping an M-bit input vector into a $2^k\binom{M}{k}$-bit vector, each of whose elements is the result of evaluating an element of T on the raw input vector.

Let s_0 of this algorithm be the initial state, s_0, of an instance of the LARC algorithm with $2^k\binom{M}{k}$ bits. The update function will be u of LARC, with the input $F_T(i)$, and, similarly, the evaluation will be e of LARC, with the input $F_T(i)$.

Algorithm 14

The LARCKDNF algorithm

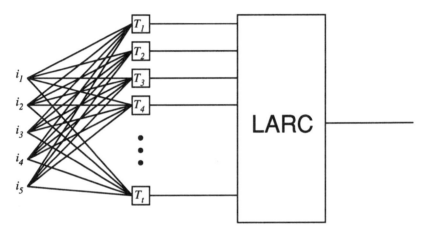

Figure 28

The LARCKDNF algorithm constructs all of the k-wide conjunctions over the inputs and their negations, then feeds them to an instance of the LARC algorithm.

of the reinforcement that the agent will gain, per trial, if it generates action a whenever term t is satisfied by the input and action $\neg a$ otherwise. The quantity $ubr_\alpha(t, a)$ is the upper bound of a $100(1 - \alpha)\%$ confidence interval on the expected reinforcement gained from performing action a whenever term t is satisfied by the input and action $\neg a$ otherwise. The formal definition is given in algorithm 15.

As in the regular interval estimation algorithm, the evaluation criterion is chosen in such a way as to make the important trade-off between acting to gain information and acting to gain reinforcement. Thus, the first requirement for a term to cause a 1 to be emitted is that the upper bound on the expected reinforcement of emitting a 1 when this term is satisfied is higher than the upper bound on the expected reinforcement of emitting a 0 when the term is satisfied.

$s_0 = $ the set T, with a collection of statistics
   associated with each member of the set

$e(s, i) = $ for each t in s
   if i satisfies t and
      $ubr_\alpha(t, 1) > ubr_\alpha(t, 0)$ and
      $\Pr(er(t, 1) = er(t, 0)) < \beta$
   then return 1
return 0

$u(s, i, a, r) = $ for each t in s
   update_term_statistics(t, i, a, r)
return s

Algorithm 15
The IEKDNF algorithm

Let the *equivalence probability* of a term be the probability that the expected reinforcement is the same no matter what choice of action is made when the term is satisfied. The second requirement for a term to cause a 1 to be emitted is that the equivalence probability be small. Without this criterion, terms for which no action is better will, roughly, alternate between choosing action 1 and action 0. Because the output of the entire algorithm will be 1 whenever any term has value 1, this alternation of values can cause a large number of wrong answers. Thus, if we can convince ourselves that a term is irrelevant by showing that its choice of action makes no difference, we can safely ignore it.

At any moment in the operation of this algorithm, we can extract a symbolic description of its current action function. It is the disjunction of all terms t such that $ubr_\alpha(t, 1) > ubr_\alpha(t, 0)$ and $\Pr(er(t, 1) = er(t, 0)) < \beta$. This is the k-DNF expression according to which the agent is choosing its actions.

In the simple Boolean reinforcement-learning scenario, the necessary statistical tests are quite simple. For each term, the following statistics are stored: n_0, the number of trials of action 0; s_0, the number of successes of action 0; n_1, the number of trials of action 1; and s_1, the number of successes of action 1. These are incremented only when the associated term is satisfied by the current input instance. Using the definition of $ub(x, n)$ from algorithm 10, we can define $ubr_\alpha(t, 0)$ as $ub(s_0, n_0)$ and $ubr_\alpha(t, 1)$ as $ub(s_1, n_1)$, where s_0, n_0, s_1, and n_1 are the statistics associated with term t and α is used in the computation of ub.

To test for equality of the underlying Bernoulli parameters, we use a two-sided test at the β level of significance that rejects the hypothesis that the parameters are equal whenever

$$\frac{\frac{s_0}{n_0} - \frac{s_1}{n_1}}{\sqrt{\frac{(\frac{s_0+s_1}{n_0+n_1})(1-\frac{s_0+s_1}{n_0+n_1})(n_0+n_1)}{n_0 n_1}}} \text{ is either } \begin{cases} \leq -z_{\beta/2} \\ \text{or} \\ \geq +z_{\beta/2} \end{cases}$$

where $z_{\beta/2}$ is a standard normal deviate [48]. Because sample size is important for this test, the algorithm is slightly modified to ensure that, at the beginning of a run, each action is chosen a minimum number of times. This parameter will be referred to as β_{min}.

As for the interval-estimation algorithm, real-valued reinforcement can be handled in IEKDNF using statistical tests appropriate for normally distributed values or for nonparametric models. In nonstationary environments, statistics can be decayed in order to ensure that the algorithm does not stay converged to a nonoptimal strategy.

The complexity of this algorithm is the same as that of the LARCKDNF algorithm of section 6.3, namely $O(M^k)$.

6.5 Empirical Comparison

This section reports the results of a set of experiments designed to compare the performance of the algorithms discussed in this chapter with one another, as well as with some other standard methods.

6.5.1 Algorithms and Environments
The following algorithms were tested in these experiments:

- LARCKDNF (algorithm 14)
- IEKDNF (algorithm 15)
- LARC (algorithm 8)
- BPRC (algorithm 9)
- IE (algorithm 10)

The regular interval-estimation algorithm IE is included as a yardstick; it is computationally much more complex than the other algorithms and may be expected to out-perform them.

Each of the algorithms was tested in three different environments. The environments are called *binomial Boolean expression worlds* and can be characterized by the parameters M, *expr*, p_{1s}, p_{1n}, p_{0s}, and p_{0n}. The parameter M is the number of input bits; *expr* is a Boolean expression over the input bits; p_{1s} is the probability of receiving reinforcement value 1 given that action 1 is taken when the input instance satisfies *expr*; p_{1n} is the probability of receiving reinforcement value 1 given that action 1 is taken when the input instance does not satisfy *expr*; p_{0s} is the probability of receiving reinforcement value 1 given that action 0 is taken when the input instance satisfies *expr*; p_{0n} is the probability of receiving reinforcement value 1 given that action 0 is taken when the input instance does not satisfy *expr*. Input vectors are chosen randomly by the world according to a uniform probability distribution.

Table 6 shows the values of these parameters for each task. The first task has a simple, linearly separable function; what makes it difficult is the small separation between the reinforcement probabilities. Task 6 has highly differentiated reinforcement probabilities, but the function to be learned is a complex exclusive-or. Finally, Task 7 is a simple conjunctive function, but all of the reinforcement probabilities are high and it has significantly more input bits than the other two tasks.

6.5.2 Parameter Tuning

Each of the algorithms has a set of parameters. For both IEKDNF and LARCKDNF, $k = 2$. Algorithms LARC and LARCKDNF have parameters α, β, and σ. Following Sutton [89], parameters β and σ in LARCKDNF and LARC are fixed to have values .1 and .3, respectively.[3] The IEKDNF algorithm has two confidence-interval parameters, $z_{\alpha/2}$ and $z_{\beta/2}$, and a minimum age for the equality test β_{min}, while the IE algorithm has only $z_{\alpha/2}$. Finally, the BPRC algorithm has a large set of parameters: β, learning rate of the evaluation output units, β_h, learning rate of the evaluation hidden units, ρ, learning rate of the action output units, and ρ_h, learning rate of the action hidden units. All of the parameters for each algorithm are chosen to optimize the behavior of that algorithm on the chosen task. The success of an algorithm is measured by the average reinforcement received per tick, averaged over the entire run.

For each algorithm and environment, a series of 100 trials of length 3000 were run with different parameter values. Table 7 shows the best set of parameter values found for each algorithm-environment pair.

Table 6
Parameters of test environments for k-DNF experiments

Task	M	expr	p_{1s}	p_{1n}	p_{0s}	p_{0n}
5	3	$(i_0 \wedge i_1) \vee (i_1 \wedge i_2)$	.6	.4	.4	.6
6	3	$(i_0 \wedge \neg i_1) \vee (i_1 \wedge \neg i_2) \vee (i_2 \wedge \neg i_0)$	.9	.1	.1	.9
7	10	$i_2 \wedge \neg i_5$	.9	.6	.5	.8

[3]This strategy seemed to work well until LARCKDNF was applied to task 7. In this situation, there are 180 inputs to the linear associator; with so many inputs, the large value of β causes the weights to grow without bound. To remedy this problem, but to avoid more parameter tuning, for task 7, β was set to the same value as α.

Table 7
Best parameter values for each k-DNF algorithm in each environment

ALG-TASK	5	6	7
LARCKDNF			
α	.125	.25	.001
IEKDNF			
$z_{\alpha/2}$	3	3.5	2.5
$z_{\beta/2}$	1	2.5	3.5
β_{min}	15	5	30
LARC			
α	.125	.0625	.03
BPRC			
β	.1	.25	.1
β_h	.2	.3	.1
ρ	.15	.15	.3
ρ_h	.2	.05	.3
IE			
$z_{\alpha/2}$	3.0	1.5	2.0

6.5.3 Results

Using the best parameter values for each algorithm and environment, the performance of the algorithms was compared on runs of length 3000. The performance metric was average reinforcement per tick, averaged over the entire run. The results are shown in table 8, together with the expected reinforcement of executing a completely random behavior (choosing actions 0 and 1 with equal probability) and of executing the optimal behavior.

As in the set of experiments described in chapter 4, we must examine the relationships of statistically significant dominance among the algorithms for each task. Figure 29 shows, for each task, a pictorial representation of the results of a 1-sided t-test applied to each pair of experimental results. The graphs encode a partial order of significant dominance, with solid lines representing significance at the .95 level.

With the best parameter values for each algorithm, it is also instructive to compare the rate at which performance improves as a function of the number of training instances. Figures 30, 31, and 32 show superimposed plots of the learning curves for each of the algorithms. Each point represents the average reinforcement received over a sequence of 100 steps, averaged over 100 runs of length 3000.

Table 8
Average reinforcement for k-DNF problems over 100 runs of length 3000

ALG-TASK	5	6	7
LARCKDNF	.5783	.8903	.7474
IEKDNF	.5789	.8900	.7939
LARC	.5456	.7459	.7644
BPRC	.5456	.7406	.7620
IE	.5827	.8966	.7205
random	.5000	.5000	.7000
optimal	.6000	.9000	.8250

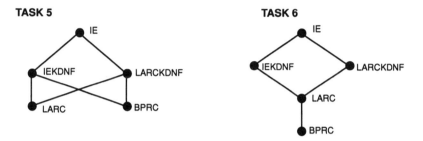

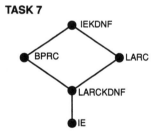

Figure 29
Significant dominance partial order among k-DNF algorithms for each task

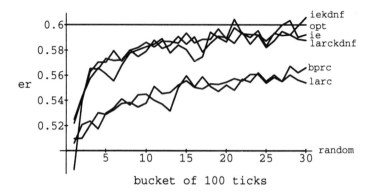

Figure 30
Learning curves for Task 5

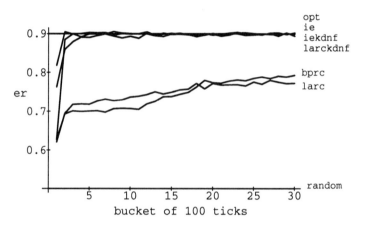

Figure 31
Learning curves for Task 6

6.5.4 Discussion

On Tasks 5 and 6, the basic interval-estimation algorithm, IE, performed significantly better than any of the other algorithms. The magnitude of its superiority, however, is not extremely great—figures 30 and 31 reveal that the IEKDNF and LARCKDNF algorithms have similar performance characteristics both to each other and to IE. On these two tasks, the overall performance of IEKDNF and LARCKDNF were not found to be significantly different.

The backpropagation algorithm, BPRC, performed considerably worse than expected on Tasks 5 and 6. It is very difficult to tune

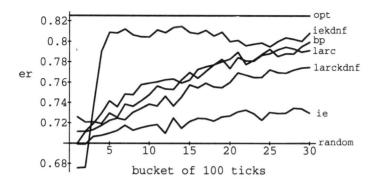

Figure 32
Learning curves for Task 7

the parameters for this algorithm, so its poor performance may be explained by a suboptimal setting of parameters.[4] However, it is possible to see in the learning curves of figures 30 and 31 that the performance of BP was still increasing at the ends of the runs. This may indicate that with more training instances it would eventually converge to optimal performance.

The LARC algorithm performed poorly on both Tasks 5 and 6. This poor performance was expected on Task 6, because linear associators are known to be unable to learn functions that are not linearly separable [62]. Task 5 is difficult for LARC because, during the execution of the algorithm, the evaluation function can be too complex to be learned by the simple linear associator, even though the action function is linearly separable.

Task 7 reveals many interesting strengths and weaknesses of the algorithms. One of the most interesting is that IE suddenly becomes the worst performer. Because the target function is simple and there is a larger number of input bits, the ability to generalize across input instances becomes crucial. The IEKDNF algorithm is able to find the correct action function early during the run (this is apparent in the learning curve of figure 32). However, because the reinforcement values are not highly differentiated and because the size of the set T is quite large, it begins to include extraneous terms due to statistical fluctuations in the environment, causing slightly degraded performance. The BPRC and LARCKDNF algorithms have very similar performance on

[4]In the parameter tuning phase, the parameters were varied independently—it may well be necessary to perform gradient-ascent search in the parameter space, but that is a computationally difficult task, especially when the evaluation of any point in parameter space may have a high degree of noise.

Task 7, with the LARC algorithm performing slightly worse, but still reasonably well. The good performance of the generalizing algorithms is especially apparent when we consider the size of the input space for this task. With 10 input bits, by the end of a run of length 3000, each input can only be expected to have been seen about 3 times. This accounts for the poor performance of IE, which would eventually reach optimal asymptotic performance on longer runs.

6.6 Conclusion

From this study, we can see that it is useful to design algorithms that are tailored to learning certain restricted classes of functions. The two specially-designed algorithms far out-performed standard methods of comparable complexity; the IEKDNF algorithm performed better than any of the available methods of any complexity on a problem with a simple action function over a large domain of inputs. In addition, the methods based on overt statistical tests converged to good strategies much more quickly than the algorithms based on artificial neural-network techniques. This may be because the statistical algorithms start without an initial bias to overcome (the initial random setting of the weights in a network provides an initial bias) and can get more "information" out of single training instances. In addition, the statistical algorithms have internal semantics that are clear and directly interpretable in the language of classical statistics. This simplifies the process of extending the algorithm to apply to other types of worlds in a principled manner.

The next chapter will explore a more flexible algorithm, motivated by these observations, that combines statistical and symbolic learning techniques.

Chapter 7

A Generate-and-Test Algorithm

This chapter describes GTRL, a highly parametrized generate-and-test algorithm for learning Boolean functions from reinforcement. Some parameter settings make it highly time- and space-efficient, but allow it to learn only a restricted class of functions; other parameter settings allow it to learn arbitrarily complex functions, but at a cost in time and space.

7.1 Introduction

The generate-and-test reinforcement-learning algorithm, GTRL, performs a bounded, real-time beam-search in the space of Boolean formulae, searching for a formula that represents an action function that exhibits high performance in the environment. This algorithm adheres to the strict synchronous tick discipline of the learning-behavior formulation of chapter 2, performing its search incrementally, while using the best available solution to generate actions for the inputs with which it is presented.

The algorithm has, at any time, a set of hypotheses under consideration. A hypothesis has as its main component a Boolean formula whose atoms are input bits or their negations. Negations can occur only at the lowest level in the formulae.[1] Each formula represents a potential action-map for the behavior, generating action 1 whenever the current input instance satisfies the formula and action 0 when it does not. The GTRL algorithm generates new hypotheses by combining the formulae of existing hypotheses using syntactic conjunction and disjunction operators.[2] This generation of new hypotheses represents a search through Boolean-formula space; statistics related to the performance of the hypotheses in the domain are used to guide the search, choosing appropriate formulae to be combined.

[1] Any Boolean formula can be put in this form using DeMorgan's laws.
[2] Other choices of syntactic search operators are possible. Conjunction and disjunction are used here because of the availability of good heuristics for guiding their application. These heuristics will be discussed in section 7.5.1.

This search is quite constrained, however. There is a limit on the number of hypotheses with formulae at each level of Boolean complexity (depth of nesting of Boolean operators), making the process very much like a beam search in which the entire beam is retained in memory. As time passes, old elements may be deleted from and new elements added to the beam, as long as the size is kept constant. This guarantees that the algorithm will operate in constant time per input instance and that the space requirement will not grow without bound over time.[3]

This search method is inspired by Schlimmer's STAGGER system [79, 80, 81, 82, 83], which learns Boolean functions from input-output pairs. STAGGER makes use of a number of techniques, including a Bayesian weight-updating component, that are inappropriate for the reinforcement-learning problem. In addition, it is not strictly limited in time- or space-complexity. The GTRL algorithm exploits STAGGER's idea of performing incremental search in the space of Boolean formulae, using statistical estimates of "necessity" and "sufficiency" (these notions will be made concrete in the following discussion) to guide the search.

The presentation of the GTRL algorithm will be initially independent of any distributional assumptions about the reinforcement values generated by the environment; it will, however, assume that the environment is consistent (see section 2.1.2 for the definition) for the agent. The process of tailoring the algorithm to work for particular kinds of reinforcement will be described in section 7.3.

7.2 High-Level Description

As with other learning algorithms, we will view the GTRL algorithm in terms of initial state, update function, and evaluation function, as shown in algorithm 16. The internal state of the GTRL algorithm consists of a set of hypotheses organized into levels. Along with a Boolean formula, each hypothesis contains a set of statistics that reflect different aspects of the performance of the formula as an action map in the domain. Each level contains hypotheses whose formulae are of a given Boolean complexity. Figure 33 shows an example GTRL internal state. Level 0 consists of hypotheses whose formulae are individual atoms corresponding to the input bits and to their negations, as well as the hypotheses whose formulae are the logical constants *true* and

---

[3]An alternative would be to simply limit the total number of hypotheses, without sorting them into levels. This approach would give added flexibility, but would also cause some increase in computational complexity. In addition, it is often beneficial to retain hypotheses at low levels of complexity because of their usefulness as building blocks.

false.[4] Hypotheses at level 1 have formulae that are conjunctions and disjunctions of the formulae of the hypotheses at level 0. In general, the hypotheses at level n have formulae that consist of conjunctions or disjunctions of two formulae: one from level $n-1$ and one from any level, from 0 to $n-1$. The hypotheses at each level are divided into working and candidate hypotheses; the reasons for this distinction will be made clear during the detailed explanation of the algorithm.

The update function of the GTRL algorithm consists of two phases: first, updating the statistics of the individual hypotheses and, second, adding and deleting hypotheses.

$s_0 =$	array $[0..L]$ of
	record
	working-hypoths: array$[0..H]$ of hypoth
	candidate-hypoths: array$[0..C]$ of hypoth
	end
$u(s, i, a, r) =$	update-hypotheses (s, i, a, r)
	for each *level* in s do begin
	add-hypotheses $(level, s)$
	promote-hypotheses $(level)$
	prune-hypotheses $(level)$
	end
$e(s, i) =$	$h :=$ best-predictor (s)
	if satisfies (i, h) then
	return 1
	else return 0

Algorithm 16
High-level description of the GTRL algorithm

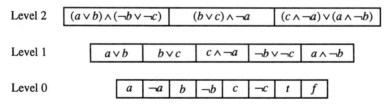

Figure 33
Example GTRL internal state

---

[4]It is necessary to include *true* and *false* in case either of those is the optimal hypothesis. Hypotheses at higher levels are simplified, so even if $a \wedge \neg a$ or $a \vee \neg a$ were to be constructed at level 1, it would not be retained.

The evaluation function also works in two phases. The first step is to find the working hypothesis at any level that has the best performance at choosing actions. If the chosen working hypothesis is satisfied by the input instance to be evaluated, action 1 is generated; if it is not satisfied, action 0 is generated.

The following sections will examine these processes in greater detail.

7.3 Statistics

Associated with each working and candidate hypothesis is a set of statistics; these statistics are used to choose working hypotheses for generating actions and for combination into new candidate hypotheses at higher levels. The algorithms for updating the statistical information and computing statistical quantities are modularly separated from the rest of the GTRL algorithm. The choice of statistical module will depend on the distribution of reinforcement values received from the environment. Appendix A provides the detailed definitions of statistics modules for cases in which the reinforcement values are binomially or normally distributed; in addition, it contains a nonparametric statistics module for use when there is no known model of the distribution of reinforcement values. A statistics module supplies the following functions:

$age(h)$:   The number of times the behavior, as a whole, has taken the action that would have been taken had hypothesis h been used to generate the action.

$er(h)$:   A point estimate of the expected reinforcement received given that the action taken by the behavior agrees with the one that would have been generated had hypothesis h been used to generate the action.

$er\text{-}ub(h)$:   The upper bound of a $100(1 - \alpha)\%$ confidence interval estimate of the quantity estimated by $er(h)$.

$erp(h)$:   A point estimate of the expected reinforcement received given that hypothesis h was used to generate the action that resulted in the reinforcement.

$erp\text{-}ub(h)$:   The upper bound of a $100(1 - \alpha)\%$ confidence interval estimate of the quantity estimated by $erp(h)$.

$N(h)$:   A statistical measure of the probability that the expected reinforcement of executing action 0 when hypothesis h is not satisfied is greater than the expected reinforcement of execution action 1 when hypothesis h is not satisfied.

$S(h)$:   A statistical measure of the probability that the expected reinforcement of executing action 1 when hypothesis h is

satisfied is greater than the expected reinforcement of executing action 0 when hypothesis h is satisfied.

7.4 Evaluating Inputs

Each time the evaluation function is called, the most predictive working hypothesis is chosen by taking the one with the highest value of
prediction value pv, defined as

$$pv(h) = \lfloor \kappa \ er(h) \rfloor + erp\text{-}ub(h) \ .$$

This definition has the effect of sorting first on the value of *er*, then
breaking ties based on the value of *erp-ub*. The constant multiplier κ
can be adjusted to make this criterion more or less sensitive to low-
order digits of the value of $er(h)$.[5]

What makes this an appropriate criterion for choosing the hypothesis with the best performance? The quantity that most clearly represents the predictive value of the hypothesis is $erp(h)$, which is a
point estimate of the expected reinforcement given that actions are
chosen according to hypothesis h. Unfortunately, this quantity only
has a useful value after the hypothesis has been chosen to generate
actions a number of times. Thus, as in the interval estimation algorithm, we make use of $erp\text{-}ub(h)$, the upper bound of a confidence
interval estimate of the expected reinforcement of acting according to
hypothesis h.

So, why not simply choose the working hypothesis with the highest value of $erp\text{-}ub(h)$, similar to the execution of the interval estimation algorithm? The reason lies in the fact that in the GTRL algorithm,
new hypotheses are continually being created. If the algorithm always
chooses hypotheses with high values of $erp\text{-}ub(h)$, it will be in danger
of spending nearly all of its time choosing hypotheses because little
is known about them, rather than because they are known to perform well. The value of $er(h)$ serves as a filter on hypotheses that will
prevent much of this fruitless exploration. The quantity $er(h)$ is not a
completely accurate estimator of $erp(h)$, because the distribution of instances over which it is defined may be different than the distribution
of input instances presented to the entire algorithm,[6] but it serves as
a useful approximation. We can use $er(h)$ rather than $er\text{-}ub(h)$ because
the statistics used to compute $er(h)$ get updated even when h is not

---

[5]In all of the experiments described in this chapter, κ had the value 1000.
[6]This difference in distributions depends on the fact that $er(h)$ is conditioned on the
agreement between hypothesis h and whatever hypotheses are actually being used to
generate actions.

used to generate actions, so that the statistic becomes valid eventually without having to do any special work. Thus, hypotheses that look good on the basis of the value of $er(h)$ tend to get chosen to act; as they do, the value of $erp\text{-}ub(h)$ begins to reflect their true predictive value. This method still spends some time acting according to untested hypotheses, but that is necessary in order to allow the algorithm to discover the correct hypothesis initially and to adjust to a dynamically changing world. The amount of exploration that actually takes place can be controlled by changing the rate at which new hypotheses are generated, as will be discussed in section 7.7.

Once a working hypothesis is chosen, it is used to evaluate the input instance. An input vector i satisfies hypothesis h if h's formula evaluates to *true* under the valuation of the atoms supplied by input i. If the input instance satisfies the chosen hypothesis, action 1 is generated; otherwise, action 0 is generated.

7.5 Managing Hypotheses

The process by which hypotheses are managed in the GTRL algorithm can be divided into three parts: adding, promoting, and pruning. On each call to the update function, the statistics of all working and candidate hypotheses are updated. Then, if it is time to do so, a new hypothesis may be constructed and added to the candidate list of some level. Candidate hypotheses that satisfy the appropriate requirements are "promoted" to be working hypotheses. Finally, any level that has more working hypotheses than the constant number allotted to it will have its working hypothesis list pruned.

7.5.1 Adding Hypotheses

Search in the GTRL algorithm is carried out by adding hypotheses. Each new hypothesis is a conjunction or disjunction of hypotheses from lower levels.[7] On each update cycle, a candidate hypothesis is added to a level if the level is not yet fully populated (the total number of working and candidate hypotheses is less than the maximum number of working hypotheses) or if it has been a certain length of time since a candidate hypothesis was last generated for this level and there is room for a new candidate.

---

[7]Terminology is being abused here in order to simplify the presentation. Rather than conjoining hypotheses, the algorithm actually creates a new hypothesis whose formula is the conjunction of the formulae of the operand hypotheses. This use of terminology should not cause any confusion.

If it is time to generate a new hypothesis, it is randomly decided whether to make a conjunctive or disjunctive hypothesis.[8] Once the combining operator is determined, operands must be chosen.

The following search heuristic is used to guide the selection of operands:

> When making a conjunction, use operands that have a high value of necessity; when making a disjunction, use operands that have a high value of sufficiency.

The terms *necessity* and *sufficiency* have a standard logical interpretation: P is sufficient for Q if P implies Q; P is necessary for Q if $\neg P$ implies $\neg Q$ (that is, Q implies P). Schlimmer follows Duda, Hart, and Nilsson [26, 27], defining the logical sufficiency of evidence E for hypothesis H as

$$LS(E, H) = \frac{\Pr(E \mid H)}{\Pr(E \mid \neg H)}$$

and the logical necessity of E for H as

$$LN(E, H) = \frac{\Pr(\neg E \mid H)}{\Pr(\neg E \mid \neg H)} \ .$$

If E is truly logically sufficient for H, then E implies H, so $\Pr(E \mid \neg H) = 0$, making $LS(E, H) = \infty$. If E and H are statistically independent, then $LS(E, H) = 1$. Similarly, if E is logically necessary for H, then $\neg E$ implies $\neg H$, so $\Pr(\neg E \mid H) = 0$, making $LN(E, H) = 0$. As before, if E and H are independent, $LN(E, H) = 1$.

What makes functions like these useful for our purposes is that they encode the notions of "degree of implication" and "degree of implication by."[9] Let $h^*(i)$ be the optimal hypothesis, that is, the action map that has the highest expected instantaneous reinforcement in the domain. We would like to use these same notions of necessity and sufficiency to guide our search, estimating the necessity and sufficiency of hypotheses in the GTRL algorithm state for h^*, the Boolean

---

[8]Schlimmer's STAGGER system generates new hypotheses in response to errors, using the nature of the error (false positive vs. true negative) to determine whether the new hypothesis should be a conjunction or a disjunction. This method cannot be applied in the general reinforcement-learning scenario, in which the algorithm is never told what the "correct" answer is, making it unable to know whether or not it just made an "error."

[9]The LS and LN functions were designed for combining evidence in a human-intuitive way; their quantitative properties are crucial to their correctness and usefulness for this purpose. The S and N operators that will be proposed do not have the appropriate quantitative properties for such uses.

function that encodes the optimal action policy for the environment. But, because of the reinforcement-learning setting of our problem, we have no access to or direct information about h^*—the environment never tells the agent which action it *should* have taken.

Let us first consider an appropriate measure of sufficiency. By the definition of conditional probability, we can rewrite the definition of logical sufficiency as

$$LS(E, H) = \frac{Pr(E \mid H)}{Pr(E \mid \neg H)}$$
$$= \frac{Pr(E \wedge H) Pr(\neg H)}{Pr(E \wedge \neg H) Pr(H)}$$
$$= \frac{Pr(H \mid E) Pr(\neg H)}{Pr(\neg H \mid E) Pr(H)} \; .$$

We are interested in the sufficiency of a particular hypothesis, h, for the optimal hypothesis, h^*, or $LS(h, h^*)$, which is equal to

$$\frac{Pr(h^* \mid h) Pr(\neg h^*)}{Pr(\neg h^* \mid h) Pr(h^*)} \; .$$

It is easiest to consider the case of deterministic Boolean reinforcement first. In this case, $Pr(h^* \mid h) = Pr(r = 1 \mid a = 1 \wedge h)$, which is the same as the expected reinforcement of executing action 1 given that h is satisfied, or $er(1 \mid h)$. So, we can express logical sufficiency as

$$LS(h, h^*) = \frac{er(1 \mid h)}{er(0 \mid h)} \cdot \frac{Pr(\neg h^*)}{Pr(h^*)} \; .$$

There are two further steps that we will take to derive our heuristic measure of sufficiency. The first is to notice that the term $Pr(\neg h^*)/Pr(h^*)$ will occur in the sufficiency of every hypothesis h, and so may be eliminated without changing the ordering induced by the sufficiency function. The next step is to generalize this formulation to the case in which the world may be nondeterministic and reinforcement non-Boolean. In such cases, the expected reinforcement values may be negative, making the ratio an inappropriate measure of their relative magnitudes. Instead, we will define sufficiency as

$$S(h) = Pr(er(1 \mid h) > er(0 \mid h)) \; .$$

This measure is strongly related to the difference of the two expected reinforcements, but is much more stable when estimates of the quantity are constructed on line. Any function that induces the same ordering on hypotheses may be used in place of S; in particular, if a statistical test such as Student's t is used, the raw t values may be used directly without translation back into the probability domain. Necessity can be analogously defined to be

$$N(h) = \Pr(er(0 \mid \neg h) > er(1 \mid \neg h)) \ .$$

Now we understand the definition and purpose of the necessity and sufficiency operators, but what makes them appropriate for use as search-control heuristics? In general, if we have a hypothesis that is highly sufficient, it can be best improved by making it highly necessary as well; this can be achieved by making the hypothesis more general by disjoining it with another sufficient hypothesis. Similarly, given a highly necessary hypothesis, we would like to make it more sufficient; we can achieve this through specialization by conjoining it with another necessary hypothesis. As a simple example, consider the case in which $h^* = a \lor b$. In this case, the hypothesis a is logically sufficient for h^*, so the heuristic will have us try to improve it by disjoining it with another sufficient hypothesis. If $h^* = a \land b$, the hypothesis a is logically necessary for h^*, so the heuristic would give preference to conjoining it with another necessary hypothesis.

Having decided, for instance, to create a new disjunctive hypothesis at level n, the algorithm uses sufficiency as a criterion for choosing operands. This is done by creating two sorted lists of hypotheses: the first list consists of the hypotheses of level $n - 1$, sorted from highest to lowest sufficiency; the second list contains all of the hypotheses from levels 0 to $n - 1$, also sorted by sufficiency. The first list is limited in order to allow complete coverage of the search space without duplication of hypotheses at different levels. Thus, for example, a hypothesis of depth 2 can be constructed at level 2, but one of depth 1 cannot.

Given the two sorted lists (another sorting criterion could easily be substituted for necessity or sufficiency at this point), a new disjunctive hypothesis is constructed by syntactically disjoining the formulae associated with the hypotheses at the top of each list. This new formula is then simplified and put into a canonical form.[10] If the simplified formula is of depth less than n it is discarded, because if it is important, it will occur at a lower level and we wish to avoid duplication.

---

[10]The choice of canonicalization and simplification procedures represents a tradeoff between computation time and space used in canonicalization against the likelihood that duplicate hypotheses will not be detected. Any process for putting Boolean formulae into a normal form that reduces semantic equivalence to syntactic equivalence has exponential worst-case time and space complexity in the original size of the formula. The GTRL algorithm currently uses a very basic simplification process whose complexity is linear in the original size of the formula and that seems, empirically, to work well. This simplification process is described in detail in appendix B.

If it is of depth n, it is tested for syntactic equality against all other hypotheses at level n. If the hypothesis is not a syntactic duplicate, it is added to the candidate list of level n and its statistics are initialized. If the new hypothesis is too simple or is a duplicate, two new indices into the sorted lists are chosen and the process is repeated. The new indices are chosen so that the algorithm finds the nonduplicate disjunction made from a pair of hypotheses whose sum of indices is least. The complexity of this process can be controlled by limiting the total number of new hypotheses that can be tried before giving up. In addition, given such a limit, it is possible to generate only prefixes of the sorted operand-lists that are long enough to support the desired number of attempts.

7.5.2 Promoting Hypotheses

On each update phase, the candidate hypotheses are considered for promotion. The reason for dividing the candidate hypotheses from the working hypotheses is to be sure that they have gathered enough statistics for their values of the statistics N, S, and er to be fairly accurate before they enter the pool from which operands and the action-generating hypothesis are chosen. Thus, the criterion for promotion is simply the age of the hypothesis, which reflects the accuracy of its statistics. Any candidate that is old enough is moved, on this phase, to the working hypothesis list.

7.5.3 Pruning Hypotheses

After candidates have been promoted, the total number of working hypotheses in a level may exceed the preset limit. If this happens, the working hypothesis list for the level is pruned. A hypothesis can play an important role in the GTRL algorithm for any of three reasons: its prediction value is high, making it useful for choosing actions; its sufficiency is high, making it useful for combining into disjunctions; or its necessity is high, making it useful for combining into conjunctions. For these reasons, we adopt the following pruning strategy:

> To prune down to n hypotheses, first choose the n/3 hypotheses with the highest predictive value; of the remaining hypotheses, choose the n/3 with the highest necessity; and, finally, of the remaining hypotheses, choose the n/3 with the highest sufficiency.

This pruning criterion is applied to all but the bottommost and topmost levels. Level 0, which contains the atomic hypotheses and their negations, must never be pruned, or the capability of generating the whole space of fixed-size Boolean formulae will be lost. Because its hypotheses will not undergo further recombination, the top level is pruned so as to retain the n most predictive hypotheses.

7.6 Parameters of the Algorithm

The GTRL algorithm is highly configurable, with its complexity and learning ability controlled by the following parameters:

L: The number of levels of hypotheses.

$z_{\alpha/2}$:   The size of the confidence interval used to generate *erp-ub*.

$H(l)$:   The maximum number of working hypotheses per level; can be a function of level number, l.

$C(l)$:   The maximum number of candidate hypotheses per level; can be a function of level number, l.

PA: The age at which candidate hypotheses are promoted to be working hypotheses.

R: The rate at which new hypotheses are generated; every R ticks, for each level, l, if there are not more than $C(l)$ candidate hypotheses, a new one is generated.

T: The maximum number of new hypotheses that are tried, in a tick, to find a nonduplicate hypothesis.

M: The number of input bits.

Because level 0 is fixed, we have $H(0) = 2M + 2$.

7.7 Computational Complexity

The space complexity of the GTRL algorithm is

$$O\left(\sum_{j=0}^{L}(H(j) + C(j))2^j\right) \; ;$$

for each level j of the L levels, there are $H(j) + C(j)$ working and candidate hypotheses, each of which has size at most 2^j for the Boolean expression, plus a constant amount of space for storing the statistics associated with the hypothesis. This expression can be simplified, if H and C are independent of level, to

$$O(L(H + C)(2^{L+1} - 1)) \; .$$

which is

$$O(L(H + C)2^L) \; .$$

The time complexity for the evaluation function is

$$O\left(\sum_{j=0}^{L} H(j) + 2^L\right) \; ;$$

the first term accounts for spending a constant amount of time examining each working hypothesis to see which one has the highest predictive value. Once the most predictive working hypothesis is chosen, it must be tested for satisfaction by the input instance; this process takes time proportional to the size of the expression, the maximum possible value of which is 2^L. If H is independent of level, this simplifies to

$$O(LH + 2^L) \; .$$

The expression for computation time of the update function is considerably more complex. It is the sum of the time taken to update the statistics of all the working and candidate hypotheses plus, for each level, the time to add hypotheses, promote hypotheses, and prune hypotheses for the level.

The time to update the hypotheses is the sum of the times to update the individual hypotheses. The update phase requires that each hypothesis be tested to see if it is satisfied by the input. This testing requires time proportional to the size of the hypothesis. Thus we have a time complexity of

$$O\left(\sum_{j=0}^{L} (H(j) + C(j))2^j\right)$$

which simplifies to

$$O(L(H + C)2^L) \; .$$

The time to add hypotheses consists of the time to create the two sorted lists (assumed to be done in $n \log n$ time in the length of the list) plus the number of new hypotheses tried times the amount of time to construct and test a new hypothesis for duplication. This time is, for level j,

$$O(H(j-1) \log H(j-1) + \left(\sum_{k=0}^{j-1} H(k)\right) \log\left(\sum_{k=0}^{j-1} H(k)\right)$$
$$+ T2^j(H(j) + C(j))) \; .$$

The last term is the time for testing new hypotheses against old ones at the same level to be sure there are no duplicates. Testing for syntactic equality takes time proportional to the size of the hypothesis and must be done against all working and candidate hypotheses in level j. There is no explicit term for simplification of newly created hypotheses because GTRL uses a procedure that is linear in the size of the hypothesis.

The time to promote hypotheses is simply proportional to the number of candidates, $C(j)$.

Finally, the time to prune hypotheses is 3 times the time to choose the $H(j)/3$ best hypotheses which, for the purpose of developing upper bounds, is $H(j) \log H(j)$.

Summing these expressions for adding, promoting, and pruning at each level, and making the simplifying assumption that H and C do not vary with level yields a time complexity of

$$O(L(H \log H + LH \log(LH) + T2^L(H + C) + C + H \log H)) ,$$

which can be further simplified to

$$O(L^2 H \log(LH) + T2^L L(H + C)) . \tag{10}$$

The time complexity of the statistical update component, $O(L(H + C)2^L)$, is dominated by the second term above, making expression 10 the time complexity of the entire update function. This is the complexity of the longest possible tick. The addition and pruning of hypotheses, which are the most time-consuming steps, will happen only once every R ticks. Taking this into account, we get a kind of "average worst-case" total complexity (the average is guaranteed when taken over a number of ticks, rather than being a kind of expected complexity based on assumptions about the distribution of inputs) of

$$O(L(H + C)2^L + \frac{1}{R}L^2 H \log(LH) + \frac{T}{R}2^L L(H + C)) .$$

The complexity in the individual parameters is $O(2^L)$, $O(H \log H)$, $O(1/R)$, $O(T)$, $O(C)$. Clearly, the number of levels and the number of hypotheses per level have the greatest effect on total algorithmic complexity. This complexity is not as bad as it may look, because 2^L is just the length of the longest formula that can be constructed by the algorithm. The time and space complexities are linear in this length.

7.8 Choosing Parameter Values

This section will explore the relationship between the settings of parameter values and the learning abilities of the GTRL algorithm.

7.8.1 Number of Levels

Any Boolean function can be written with a wide variety of syntactic expressions. Consider the set of Boolean formulae with the negations driven in as far as possible, using DeMorgan's laws. The *depth* of such a formula is the maximum nesting depth of binary conjunction and disjunction operators within the formula. The *depth* of a Boolean function is defined to be the depth of the shallowest Boolean formula that expresses the function.

An instance of the GTRL algorithm with L levels of combination is unable to learn functions with depth greater than L. Whether it can learn all functions of depth L or less depends on the settings of other parameters in the algorithm. The time and space complexities of the algorithm are, technically, most sensitive to this parameter, both being exponential in the number of levels.

7.8.2 Number of Working and Candidate Hypotheses

The choice of the size of the hypothesis lists at each level also has a great effect on the overall complexity of the algorithm. The working hypothesis list needs to be at least big enough to hold all of the subexpressions of some formula that describes the target function. Thus, in order to learn the function described by $i_0 \wedge (i_1 \vee i_2) \wedge (i_3 \vee \neg i_4)$, level 1 must have room for at least two working hypotheses, $i_1 \vee i_2$ and $i_2 \vee \neg i_4$, and levels 2 and 3 must have room for at least one working hypothesis each.

This amount of space will rarely be sufficient, however. There must also be room for newly generated hypotheses to stay until they are tested and proven or disproven by their performance in the environment. Exactly how much room this is depends on the rate, R, at which new hypotheses are generated and on the size, $z_{\alpha/2}$, of the confidence intervals used to generate *erp-ub*. To see this, consider the case in which a representation of the optimal hypothesis, h^*, has already been constructed. The algorithm continues to generate new hypotheses, one every R ticks, with each new hypothesis requiring an average of j ticks to be proven to be worse than h^*. That means there must be an average of R/j slots for extra hypotheses at this level. Of course, it is likely that during the course of a run, certain nonoptimal hypotheses will take more than j ticks to disprove. This can cause h^* to be driven out of the hypothesis list altogether during the pruning phase. Thus, a more conservative strategy is to prevent this by increasing the size of the hypothesis lists, but it incurs a penalty in computation time.

Even when there is enough space for all subexpressions and their competitors at each level, it is possible for the size of the hypothesis lists to affect the speed at which the optimal hypothesis is generated by the algorithm. This can be easily understood in the context of the difficulty of a function for the algorithm. Functions whose subexpressions are not naturally preferred by the necessity and sufficiency search heuristics are difficult for the GTRL algorithm to construct. In such cases, the algorithm is reduced to randomly choosing expressions at each level.

Consider the case in which $h^* = (i_0 \wedge \neg i_1) \vee (\neg i_0 \wedge i_1)$, an exclusive-or function. Because h^* neither implies nor is implied by any of the input bits, the atoms will all have similar, average values of N and S. Due to random fluctuations in the environment, different atoms will have higher values of N and S at different times during a run. Thus, the conjunctions and disjunctions at level 1 will represent a sort of random search through expression space. This random search will eventually generate one of the following expressions: $i_0 \wedge \neg i_1$, $\neg i_0 \wedge i_1$, $i_0 \vee i_1$, $\neg i_0 \vee \neg i_1$. When one of these is generated, it will be retained in the level 1 hypothesis list because of its high necessity or sufficiency. We need only wait until the random combination process generates its companion subexpression, then they will be combined into a representation of h^* at level 2.

Even with very small hypothesis lists, the correct answer will eventually be generated. However, as problems become more difficult, the probability that the random process will, on any given tick, generate the appropriate operands becomes very small, making the algorithm arbitrarily slow to converge to the correct answer. This process can be made to take fewer ticks by increasing the size of the hypothesis list. In the limit, the hypothesis list will be large enough to hold all conjunctions and disjunctions of atoms at the previous level and as soon as it is filled, the correct building blocks for the next level will be available and apparent.

7.8.3 Promotion Age

The choice of values for the age parameter depends on how long it takes for the er, N, and S statistics to come to be a good indication of the values they are estimating. If reinforcement has a high variance, for instance, it may take more examples to get a true statistical picture of the underlying processes. If the value of R is large, causing new combinations to be made infrequently, it is often important for promotion age to be large, ensuring that the data that guides the combinations is accurate. If R is small, the effect of occasional bad combinations is not so great and may be outweighed by the advantage of moving candidate hypotheses more quickly to the working hypothesis list.

7.8.4 Rate of Generating Hypotheses

The more frequently new hypotheses are generated, the sooner the algorithm will construct important subexpressions and the more closely it will track a changing environment. However, each new hypothesis that has a promising value of er will be executed a number of times to see if its value of erp is as high as that of the current best hypothesis. In general, most of these hypotheses will not be as good as the best existing one, so using them to choose actions will decrease the algorithm's overall performance significantly.

7.8.5 Maximum New Hypothesis Tries

The attempt to make a new hypothesis can fail for two reasons. Either the newly created hypothesis already exists in the working or candidate hypothesis list of the level for which it was created or the expression associated with the hypothesis was subject to one of the reductions of appendix B, causing it to be inappropriate for this level. It is possible, but very unlikely, to have more than $H + C$ failures of the first type. The number of failures of the second type is harder to quantify.

7.9 Empirical Results

This section describes a set of experiments with the GTRL algorithm. First, the operation of the GTRL algorithm is illustrated by discussing a sample run. Then, the dependence of the algorithm's performance on the settings of its parameters is explored. Finally, the performance of the GTRL algorithm is compared with the algorithms of the previous chapter on Tasks 5, 6, and 7.

7.9.1 Sample Run

Figure 34 shows the trace of a sample run of the GTRL algorithm. It is executed on Task 8, a binomial Boolean-expression world[11] with 3 input bits, in which the expression is $(b_0 \vee b_1) \wedge (b_1 \vee b_2)$, $p_{1s} = .9$, $p_{1n} = .1$, $p_{0s} = .1$, and $p_{0n} = .9$. The figure shows the state of the algorithm at ticks 50, 100, and 250. The report for each tick shows the working hypotheses for each level, together with their statistics.[12] In order to save space in the figure, only the four most predictive working hypotheses are shown at each level. At tick 50, the two component hypotheses, $b_0 \wedge b_1$ and $b_1 \wedge b_2$, have been constructed.

---

[11] Binomial Boolean-expression worlds are defined in section 6.5.1.

[12] The age statistic reported in the trace is the number of times the hypothesis has been chosen to generate actions, rather than the value of age, which is the number of times this hypothesis has agreed with the ones that have been chosen to generate actions.

Table 9
Best parameter values for GTRL on Tasks 5, 6, and 7 from chapter 6

Task/Param	PA	R	H	Results
5	35	200	30	.5667
6	10	100	30	.7968
7	25	450	20	.7986

They both have high levels of sufficiency, which makes them good operands for disjunction. By tick 100, the correct disjunction has been made, and the most predictive hypothesis is the optimal hypothesis $(b_0 \land b_1) \lor (b_1 \land b_2)$. At tick 250, the optimal hypothesis is still winning and the average reinforcement is approaching optimal.

7.9.2 Effects of Parameter Settings on Performance

The section describes a set of experiments that illustrate how learning performance varies as a function of the values of the parameters PA, R, and H on Task 8, which was described in the previous section. The parameter L was set to 3, $z_{\alpha/2}$ to 2, C to be equal to H, and T to 100. Figures 35, 36, and 37 show the results, plotting average reinforcement per tick on 100 runs of length 3000 against each of the remaining parameters, PA, R, and H.

The expected reinforcement is maximized at a low value of PA, the promotion age of candidate hypotheses, because it is relatively easy to discriminate between good and bad actions in Task 8. When the probabilities of receiving reinforcement value 1 are closer to one another, as they are in the tasks discussed in the next section, it becomes necessary to use higher values of PA. Because this task (and all of the others discussed in this chapter) is stationary, the only reason to have a low value of R, the inverse of the rate at which new hypotheses are generated, is if the function is very difficult and hypothesis list is too small to hold all subexpressions at once. This is not the case for Task 8, so high values of R are desirable. Finally, performance increases with the length of the hypothesis lists, H, in every task. Because this task is relatively easy, however, the correct answer is usually found fairly quickly with even small values of H, so the increase is not dramatic (this is evidenced by the small range of er in figure 37.)

7.9.3 Comparison with Other Algorithms

The GTRL algorithm was tested on Tasks 5, 6, and 7 from chapter 6. The best values of the parameters for each task were determined through extensive testing, and are shown in table 9. Some of the values are arbitrarily cut off where the parameter testing stopped. For instance,

```
****** Tick   50 Summary ******
----Level 0----
PV = 897.950 EPPUB = 0.95 EP = 0.90 N =  5.02 S =  2.87 AGE =  21 H: 1
PV = 843.000 EPPUB = 1.00 EP = 0.84 N =  1.16 S =  0.59 AGE =   0 H: 0
PV = 783.000 EPPUB = 1.00 EP = 0.78 N =  0.64 S =  0.00 AGE =   0 H: f
PV = 775.000 EPPUB = 1.00 EP = 0.77 N =  0.92 S =  0.00 AGE =   2 H: 2
----Level 1----
PV = 917.000 EPPUB = 1.00 EP = 0.92 N = -1.10 S = ***** AGE =   1 H: (and 0 1)
PV = 910.000 EPPUB = 1.00 EP = 0.91 N =  0.00 S =  1.67 AGE =   0 H: (or 1 (not 2))
PV = 876.000 EPPUB = 1.00 EP = 0.87 N =  0.00 S =  1.08 AGE =   0 H: (or 1 (not 0))
PV = 870.000 EPPUB = 1.00 EP = 0.87 N =  0.00 S =  1.37 AGE =   0 H: (or 1 2)
----Level 2----
PV =1001.000 EPPUB = 1.00 EP = 1.00 N =  0.00 S =  2.45 AGE =   0 H: (or (not 0) (or 1 2))
PV = 819.000 EPPUB = 1.00 EP = 0.82 N = -1.67 S = ***** AGE =   0 H: (and (and 1 2) (or 1 2))
*** Reinf = (   37 /    50)   74.00%  Long term = (   37 /    50)   74.00% ***


****** Tick  100 Summary ******
----Level 0----
PV = 916.950 EPPUB = 0.95 EP = 0.92 N =  6.95 S =  1.87 AGE =  21 H: 1
PV = 904.000 EPPUB = 1.00 EP = 0.90 N =  2.54 S =  0.89 AGE =   0 H: 0
PV = 858.000 EPPUB = 1.00 EP = 0.86 N =  0.95 S =  0.00 AGE =   0 H: f
PV = 853.000 EPPUB = 1.00 EP = 0.85 N =  1.50 S = -0.28 AGE =   2 H: 2
----Level 1----
PV = 942.000 EPPUB = 1.00 EP = 0.94 N =  1.16 S = ***** AGE =   7 H: (and 0 1)
PV = 938.917 EPPUB = 0.92 EP = 0.94 N =  0.00 S =  1.57 AGE =   7 H: (or 0 1)
PV = 922.000 EPPUB = 1.00 EP = 0.92 N =  0.37 S =  1.12 AGE =   0 H: (and 0 2)
PV = 921.882 EPPUB = 0.88 EP = 0.92 N =  1.52 S = 23.49 AGE =   5 H: (and 1 2)
----Level 2----
PV = 976.994 EPPUB = 0.99 EP = 0.98 N = 23.49 S =  0.00 AGE =  32 H: (or (and 0 1) (and 1 2))
PV = 949.000 EPPUB = 1.00 EP = 0.95 N = 20.49 S = -1.03 AGE =   0 H: (or (and 1 2) (and 1 (not 2)))
PV = 945.000 EPPUB = 1.00 EP = 0.94 N =  1.15 S = -1.04 AGE =   1 H: (or (and 0 1) (and 1 (not 2)))
PV = 942.000 EPPUB = 1.00 EP = 0.94 N =  0.88 S = ***** AGE =   0 H: (and 0 (and 1 2))
*** Reinf = (   45 /    50)   90.00%  Long term = (   82 /   100)   82.00% ***


****** Tick  250 Summary ******
----Level 0----
PV = 906.000 EPPUB = 1.00 EP = 0.91 N =  2.38 S =  1.14 AGE =   0 H: 0
PV = 902.950 EPPUB = 0.95 EP = 0.90 N =  8.15 S =  1.90 AGE =  21 H: 1
PV = 873.000 EPPUB = 1.00 EP = 0.87 N =  1.64 S =  0.08 AGE =   2 H: 2
PV = 872.000 EPPUB = 1.00 EP = 0.87 N =  0.96 S =  0.00 AGE =   0 H: f
```

```
----Level 1----
PV = 917.831 EPPUB = 0.83 EP = 0.92 N =  0.00 S =  1.49 AGE =  10 H: (or 0 1)
PV = 907.000 EPPUB = 1.00 EP = 0.91 N =  1.45 S = 33.23 AGE =   7 H: (and 0 1)
PV = 902.882 EPPUB = 0.88 EP = 0.90 N =  1.62 S = 25.69 AGE =   5 H: (and 1 2)
PV = 895.000 EPPUB = 1.00 EP = 0.89 N =  0.42 S =  0.72 AGE =   0 H: (and 0 2)
----Level 2----
PV = 920.941 EPPUB = 0.94 EP = 0.92 N = 34.12 S = 32.40 AGE = 157 H: (or (and 0 1) (and 1 2))
PV = 905.977 EPPUB = 0.98 EP = 0.91 N = 31.79 S =  0.92 AGE =   8 H: (or (and 1 2) (and 1 (not 2)))
PV = 898.000 EPPUB = 1.00 EP = 0.90 N = 21.66 S =  0.65 AGE =   0 H: (or (and 1 2) (or 1 2))
PV = 894.962 EPPUB = 0.96 EP = 0.89 N =  0.82 S = -0.07 AGE =  15 H: (or (and 0 1) (and 1 (not 2)))
*** Reinf = (  44 /   50)  88.00% Long term = (  213 /   250)   85.20% ***
```

Figure 34
A sample run of the GTRL algorithm

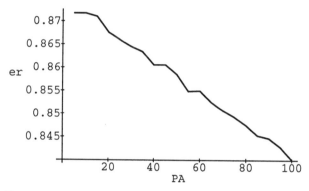

Figure 35
Performance versus parameter value PA for Task 8

performance on Task 5 might be improved with higher values of PA and performance on Task 6 would be improved with higher values of H. The average reinforcement per tick of executing GTRL at these parameter settings on 100 runs of length 3000 are shown in the final column of the table.

Figure 38 is a modified version of figure 29, with the results of the GTRL algorithm included with those of the algorithms of chapter 6 for Tasks 5, 6, and 7. On Tasks 5 and 6, the GTRL algorithm performs significantly better than the LARC and BPRC algorithms, but not as well as IE, IEKDNF, or LARCKDNF. Finally, on Task 7, the real advantage of GTRL is illustrated. On a task with a large number of inputs, GTRL finds the correct hypothesis very promptly, significantly outperforming all other algorithms.

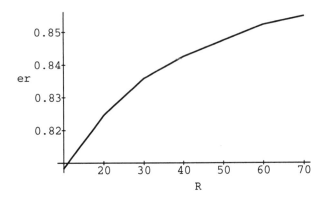

Figure 36
Performance versus parameter value R for Task 8

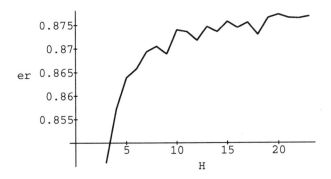

Figure 37
Performance versus parameter value H for Task 8

The learning curves of GTRL on each of the tasks are shown in figures 39, 40 and 41. They are superimposed on the learning curves of the algorithms tested in chapter 6; the GTRL curves are drawn in bold lines.

This comparison is, to some degree, unfair, because the GTRL algorithm is designed for nonstationary environments. We can see in the learning curves that, although it improves quickly early in run, it does not reach as high a steady-state level of performance as the other algorithms. It does not converge to a fixed state, because it is always entertaining new competing hypotheses. This flexibility causes a large decrease in performance. If the GTRL algorithm is to be applied in a domain in which changes, if any, are expected to take place near the

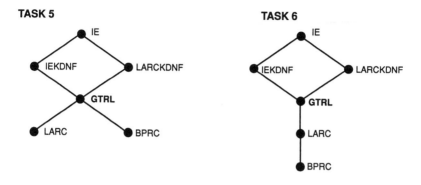

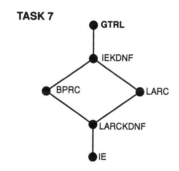

Figure 38
Significance of GTRL results on Tasks 5, 6, and 7, compared with the results of the
algorithms of chapter 6

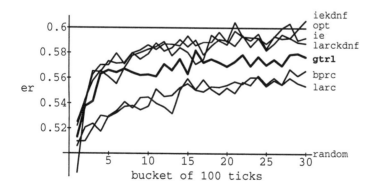

Figure 39
GTRL learning curve for Task 5 (bold) compared with the algorithms of chapter 6

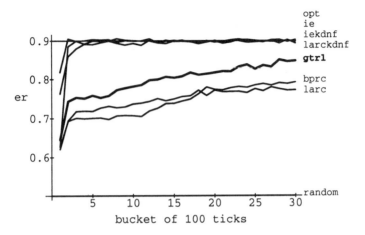

Figure 40
GTRL learning curve for Task 6 (bold) compared with the algorithms of chapter 6

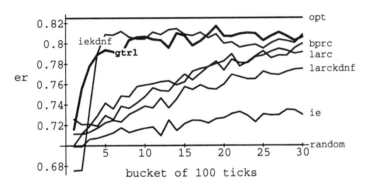

Figure 41
GTRL learning curve for Task 7 (bold) compared with the algorithms of chapter 6

beginning of a run, performance can be improved by decreasing over time the rate at which new candidate hypotheses are generated. This will cause the algorithm to spend less time experimenting and more time acting on the basis of known good hypotheses.

7.10 Conclusions

We have seen that the GTRL algorithm can be used to learn a variety of Boolean function classes with varying degrees of effectiveness and efficiency. This chapter describes only a particular instance of a general, dynamic generate-and-test method—there are a number of other possible variations.

The algorithm is designed so that other search heuristics may be easily accommodated. An example of another, potentially useful, heuristic is to combine hypotheses that are highly correlated with the optimal hypothesis. One way to implement this heuristic would be to run a linear-association algorithm, such as LARC, over the input bits and the outputs of the newly created hypotheses, then make combinations of those hypotheses that evolve large weights. It is not immediately apparent how this would compare to using the N and S heuristics.

Another possible extension would be to add genetically motivated operators, such as crossover and mutation, to the set of search operators. Many genetic methods are concerned only with the performance of the final result so this extension would have to be made carefully in order to preserve good on-line performance.

Chapter 8

Learning Action Maps with State

All of the algorithms that we have considered thus far are capable of learning only actions maps that are pure, instantaneous functions of their inputs. It is more generally the case, however, that an agent's actions must depend on the past history of input values in order to be effective. By storing information about past inputs, the agent is able to induce a finer partition on the set of world states, allowing it to make more discriminations and to tailor its actions more appropriately to the state of the world.

Perhaps the simplest way to achieve this finer-grained historical view of the world is simply to remember all input instances from the last k ticks and present them in parallel to the behavior-learning algorithm. This method has two drawbacks: it is not possible for actions to depend on conditions that reach back arbitrarily far in history and the algorithmic complexity increases considerably as the length of the available history is increased.

This chapter will present an alternative approach, based on the GTRL algorithm, that can efficiently learn simple action maps with temporal dependencies that go arbitrarily far back in history.

8.1 Set-Reset

A common component in hardware logic design is a set-reset (SR) flip-flop.[1] It has two input lines, designated *set* and *reset*, a clock, and an output line. Whenever the clock is triggered, if the *set* line is high, then the output of the unit is high; else, if the *reset* line is high, the output of the unit is low; finally, if both input lines are low, the output of the unit remains the same as it was during the previous clock cycle. The value of the output is held in the determined state until the next clock tick.

---

[1] Components of this kind are also commonly referred to as RS (reset-set) flip-flops in the logic-design literature.

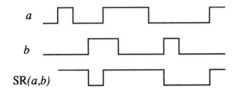

Figure 42
Timing diagram for a set-reset flip-flop

The behavior of an SR flip-flop can be described logically in terms of the following binary Boolean operator

$$SR(a, b) \equiv a \vee (\neg b \wedge \bullet SR(a, b)) \ ,$$

where $\bullet$ is the temporal operator "last." Figure 42 shows a timing diagram, in which the top two lines represent a time-history of the values of wires a and b and the bottom line represents the time history of the values of $SR(a, b)$, the output of a set-reset flip-flop whose inputs are wires a and b.

In the logical definition of SR as a Boolean operator, no initial value is specified. This problem is dealt with by adding a third logical value, $\perp$, which means, intuitively, "undefined." When an expression of the form $SR(a, b)$ is to be evaluated for the first time, it is assumed that the value of $\bullet SR(a, b)$ is $\perp$. The value $\perp$ combines with the other logical values as follows:

$$\textbf{true} \vee \perp \equiv \textbf{true}$$
$$\textbf{false} \vee \perp \equiv \perp$$
$$\perp \vee \perp \equiv \perp$$
$$\textbf{true} \wedge \perp \equiv \perp$$
$$\textbf{false} \wedge \perp \equiv \textbf{false}$$
$$\perp \wedge \perp \equiv \perp$$
$$\neg \perp \equiv \perp$$

Thus, the expression $SR(a, b)$ will have value $\perp$ until either $a \equiv \textbf{true}$, in which case $SR(a, b) \equiv \textbf{true} \vee \ldots \equiv \textbf{true}$, or $a \equiv \textbf{false}$ and $b \equiv \textbf{true}$, in which case $SR(a, b) \equiv \textbf{false} \vee (\textbf{false} \wedge \perp) \equiv \textbf{false}$.

8.2 Using SR in GTRL

In the original version of the GTRL algorithm, the hypotheses were pure Boolean functions of the input bits. This section describes an extended version of that algorithm, called GTRL-S, which has simple sequential networks as hypotheses.

8.2.1 Hypotheses

The GTRL-S algorithm is structured in exactly the same way as the GTRL algorithm. The main difference is that SR is added as another binary hypothesis-combination operator. This allows hypotheses such as

$$SR(\neg b_0, b_1 \wedge b_2) \wedge (b_1 \vee SR(SR(b_0, b_1), \neg b_2)) \ ,$$

which represents the sequential network shown in figure 43, to be constructed.

This operator does not allow every possible sequential circuit to be generated, however. In the pure-function case it was not necessary to have a negation operator because DeMorgan's laws guarantee that having access to the negated atoms is sufficient to generate any Boolean function. Unfortunately, negation cannot be moved past the SR operator in any general way, so, for instance, a sequential circuit equivalent to $\neg SR(i_0, i_1)$ cannot be generated by applications of the SR operator to atoms and their negations. This deficiency can be simply remedied by adding a unary negation operator or by adding an operator NSR, which is defined as

$$NSR(a, b) \equiv \neg SR(a, b) \ .$$

Another deficiency is that the construction of sequential networks with feedback is not allowed. Thus, the circuit shown in figure 44, which generates the sequence $0, 1, 0, 1, \ldots$, cannot be constructed. For agents embedded in realistic environments, this limitation may not be too great in practice. We would not, in general, expect such agents to have to make state changes that are not a function of changes in the world that are reflected in the agent's input vector. There is one additional limitation that is both more serious and more easily corrected. With the semantics of SR defined as they are, it is not possible to construct an expression equivalent to $\bullet a$. One way to solve this problem would be to redefine $SR(a, b)$ as $\bullet a \vee (\bullet \neg b \wedge \bullet SR(a, b))$. In that case, $\bullet a$ could be expressed as $SR(a, \neg a)$, but the search heuristics to be used in GTRL-S (described in section 8.2.3) would no longer be applicable. Another option would be to add $\bullet$ as a unary operator, along with negation. This is a reasonable course of action; it is not followed in this chapter, however, both because it would complicate the exposition and because no appropriate search heuristics for the last and negation operators are known.

In addition to the syntactic expression describing the network and the necessary statistics (discussed in section 7.3), a hypothesis also

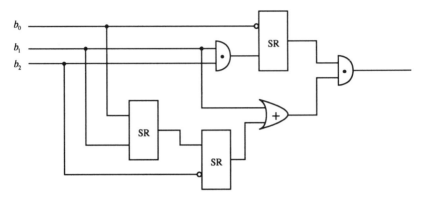

Figure 43
A sample sequential network, described by $SR(\neg b_0, b_1 \wedge b_2) \wedge (b_1 \vee SR(SR(b_0, b_1), \neg b_2)$

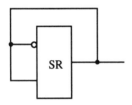

Figure 44
This circuit generates the sequence $0, 1, 0, 1, \ldots$; because it has feedback, it cannot be constructed by the GTRL-S algorithm.

contains the current *state* of each of its SR components. When a new hypothesis is created with SR as the top-level operator, that component's state is set to $\bot$. The state of SR components occurring in the operands is copied from the operand hypotheses. In order to keep all state values up to date, a new state-update phase is added to the update function. In the state-update phase, the new state of each SR component of each hypothesis is calculated as a function of the input vector and the old state, then stored back into the hypothesis. The result of this calculation may be 1, 0, or $\bot$.

Expressions containing SR operators may be partially simplified using an extension of the simplification procedure used for standard Boolean expressions. This extended simplifier is also described in appendix B.

8.2.2 Statistics
The statistical modules for GTRL-S differ from GTRL only when *satisfies*(i, h) returns the value $\bot$. In that case, none of the statistics

is updated. Once *satiofioc*(*i*, *h*) becomes defined for any input *i*, it will remain defined for every input, so this has no effect on the distribution of the instances for which statistics are collected, just on when the collection of statistics begins.

8.2.3 Search Heuristics

The problem of guiding the search for generating sequential networks is considerably more difficult than for pure functional networks. Statistics collected about the performance of expressions as generators of actions in the world are not necessarily a strong indication of their performance as the *set* or *reset* signal of an SR component. They can still provide some guidance, however.

Recall the logical definition of SR as

$$SR(a, b) \equiv a \vee (\neg b \wedge \bullet SR(a, b)) \ .$$

First, we can see that $a \rightarrow SR(a, b)$ and that $SR(a, b) \rightarrow (a \vee \neg b)$. The first observation should guide us to choose *set* operands that are sufficient for the target hypothesis. The second observation is slightly more complex, due to the fact that *set* takes precedence over *reset*, but it makes it reasonable to choose *reset* operands whose negations are necessary for the target hypothesis. From these observations we can derive the following heuristic:

> When making a set-reset hypothesis, use a *set* operand that has a high value of *sufficiency* and a *reset* operand whose negation has a high value of *necessity*.

8.2.4 Complexity

The computational complexity of the GTRL-S algorithm is the same as that of GTRL, which is discussed in section 7.7. The only additional work performed by GTRL-S is the state-update computation. It has complexity $O(L(H + C)2^L)$ (assuming that H and C are independent of level), which is of the same order as the statistical updating phase that occurs in both algorithms.

8.3 Experiments with GTRL-S

This section documents experiments with GTRL-S in some simple domains that require action mappings with state. There are no direct comparisons with other algorithms because no other directly comparable algorithms that learn action mappings with state from reinforcement are known.

```
******  Tick  100 Summary  ******
----Level 0----
PV =   666.8500 EPPUB = 0.85 EP = 0.67 N = 100.00 S =  -0.43 AGE =   4 H: (not 0)
PV =   648.7384 EPPUB = 0.74 EP = 0.65 N =   2.41 S =   4.47 AGE =  62 H: 1
PV =   633.0000 EPPUB = 1.00 EP = 0.63 N =   1.16 S =   0.00 AGE =   0 H: f
PV =   600.7935 EPPUB = 0.79 EP = 0.60 N =   0.43 S =-100.00 AGE =   1 H: 0
PV =   462.0000 EPPUB = 1.00 EP = 0.46 N =   0.00 S =  -1.16 AGE =   0 H: t
----Level 1----
PV =   619.7686 EPPUB = 0.77 EP = 0.62 N =   0.49 S =  -2.00 AGE =  19 H: (or 0 1)
PV =   619.0000 EPPUB = 1.00 EP = 0.62 N =   0.36 S =   0.00 AGE =   0 H: (and 0 1)
PV =   616.0000 EPPUB = 1.00 EP = 0.62 N =   0.94 S =   0.00 AGE =   0 H: (sr 1 (not 0) nil)
PV =   584.0000 EPPUB = 1.00 EP = 0.58 N =  -0.18 S =-100.00 AGE =   0 H: (sr 0 (not 1) nil)
*** Reinf = (   61 /   100)   61.00% Long term = (   61 /   100)   61.00% ***


******  Tick  200 Summary  ******
----Level 0----
PV =   843.9567 EPPUB = 0.96 EP = 0.84 N = 100.00 S =   2.31 AGE =  13 H: (not 0)
PV =   795.0000 EPPUB = 1.00 EP = 0.79 N =   0.00 S =   1.46 AGE =   0 H: t
PV =   765.0000 EPPUB = 1.00 EP = 0.76 N = -10.49 S =   1.00 AGE =   0 H: (not 1)
PV =   727.7384 EPPUB = 0.74 EP = 0.73 N =  -1.00 S =  10.49 AGE =  62 H: 1
PV =   705.0000 EPPUB = 1.00 EP = 0.70 N =  -1.46 S =   0.00 AGE =   0 H: f
PV =   666.7935 EPPUB = 0.79 EP = 0.67 N =  -2.31 S =-100.00 AGE =   1 H: 0
----Level 1----
PV =   912.9468 EPPUB = 0.95 EP = 0.91 N =   2.14 S =   2.83 AGE =  65 H: (sr 1 0 nil)
PV =   902.8124 EPPUB = 0.81 EP = 0.90 N =   0.87 S =   0.00 AGE =   6 H: (and 1 (not 0))
PV =   869.9690 EPPUB = 0.97 EP = 0.87 N = 100.00 S =  -0.13 AGE =  18 H: (sr (not 0) (not 1) t)
PV =   858.0000 EPPUB = 1.00 EP = 0.86 N = 100.00 S =  -0.30 AGE =   1 H: (or 1 (not 0))
PV =   857.7935 EPPUB = 0.79 EP = 0.86 N =   0.00 S =  -0.41 AGE =   1 H: (sr (not 1) 0 t)
PV =   855.0000 EPPUB = 1.00 EP = 0.85 N =   0.00 S =  -0.44 AGE =   0 H: (sr (not 0) 1 t)
*** Reinf = (   87 /   100)   87.00% Long term = (  148 /   200)   74.00% ***


******  Tick  500 Summary  ******
----Level 0----
PV =   893.9567 EPPUB = 0.96 EP = 0.89 N = 100.00 S =   2.99 AGE =  13 H: (not 0)
PV =   870.0000 EPPUB = 1.00 EP = 0.87 N =   0.00 S =   2.14 AGE =   0 H: t
PV =   864.0000 EPPUB = 1.00 EP = 0.86 N = -14.04 S =   1.99 AGE =   0 H: (not 1)
PV =   809.7384 EPPUB = 0.74 EP = 0.81 N =  -1.99 S =  14.04 AGE =  62 H: 1
PV =   799.0000 EPPUB = 1.00 EP = 0.80 N =  -2.14 S =   0.00 AGE =   0 H: f
PV =   770.7935 EPPUB = 0.79 EP = 0.77 N =  -2.99 S =-100.00 AGE =   1 H: 0
```

```
----Level 1====
PV =    904.9276 EPPUB = 0.93 EP = 0.90 N =    2.12 S =    4.85 AGE =  352 H: (sr 1 0 nil)
PV =    903.9193 EPPUB = 0.92 EP = 0.90 N = 100.00 S =    1.03 AGE =   20 H: (sr (not 0) (not 1) t)
PV =    901.0000 EPPUB = 1.00 EP = 0.90 N = 100.00 S =    0.90 AGE =    1 H: (or 1 (not 0))
PV =    894.0000 EPPUB = 1.00 EP = 0.89 N =    0.00 S =    0.59 AGE =    0 H: (sr (not 0) 1 t)
PV =    893.7935 EPPUB = 0.79 EP = 0.89 N =    0.00 S =    0.60 AGE =    1 H: (sr (not 1) 0 t)
PV =    836.9032 EPPUB = 0.90 EP = 0.84 N =   -0.74 S =    0.00 AGE =    6 H: (sr 0 (not 1) nil)
*** Reinf = (   88 /   100)  88.00%  Long term = (  415 /   500)   83.00% ***
```

Figure 45
A sample run of the GTRL-S algorithm on the simple lights and buttons problem

8.3.1 Lights and Buttons

The first domain of experimentation is very simple. It can be thought of as consisting of two light bulbs and two buttons. The input to the agent is a vector of two bits, the first having value 1 if the first light bulb is on and the second having value 1 if the second light bulb is on. The agent can generate two actions: action 0 causes the first button to be pressed and action 1 causes the second button to be pressed. One or no lights will be on at each instance. The optimal action map is to push the button corresponding to the light that is on if, in fact, a light is on. If no lights are on, the optimal action is to push the button associated with the light that was last on. A light is turned on on a given tick with probability p_l—the particular light is chosen uniformly at random. Thus, the optimal hypothesis is simply SR(b_1, b_0).

Figure 45 shows parts of the trace of a sample run of the GTRL-S algorithm in the simple lights and buttons domain, in which the correct action (as discussed above) yields reinforcement value 1 with probability .9 and the incorrect action yields reinforcement value 1 with probability .1. A light comes on each tick with probability .1. The first section of the trace shows the state of the algorithm after 100 ticks.[2] It has not yet constructed the correct hypothesis, but we can see in the statistics of the atomic hypotheses that b_1 is the most sufficient hypothesis and $\neg b_0$ is the most necessary. After 200 ticks, we can see that the correct hypothesis, SR(b_1, b_0), has just been found and appears to be the best. By tick 500, the original winning hypothesis is still at the top of the list, with another equivalent expression, SR$(\neg b_0, \neg b_1)$, being second best. The GTRL-S algorithm works quite reliably on this problem because the search heuristics provide good guidance.

---

[2]The third value in the SR expressions of the printout indicates the stored value of the unit: t for 1, nil for 0, and bottom for $\perp$ (which does not happen to occur in this trace.)

```
******  Tick   100 Summary  ******
----Level 0----
PV =   566.6504 EPPUB = 0.65 EP = 0.57 N =   1.41 S = 10.76 AGE =   45 H: (not 1)
PV =   555.6576 EPPUB = 0.66 EP = 0.56 N =   0.00 S =  4.20 AGE =    2 H: t
PV =   534.7690 EPPUB = 0.77 EP = 0.53 N = -4.47 S =  3.65 AGE =   16 H: (not 0)
PV =   358.0000 EPPUB = 1.00 EP = 0.36 N = -3.65 S =  4.47 AGE =    0 H: 0
----Level 1----
PV =   882.9699 EPPUB = 0.97 EP = 0.88 N =   1.08 S =  0.00 AGE =    6 H: (sr 0 1 t)
PV =   840.9285 EPPUB = 0.93 EP = 0.84 N =   0.00 S =  0.00 AGE =    8 H: (sr (not 1) (not 0) t)
PV =   834.0000 EPPUB = 1.00 EP = 0.83 N =   0.00 S =  0.00 AGE =    0 H: (or 0 (not 1))
PV =   532.7935 EPPUB = 0.79 EP = 0.53 N =   0.00 S =  0.09 AGE =    1 H: (or (not 0) (not 1))
----Level 0----
PV =   566.6447 EPPUB = 0.64 EP = 0.57 N = 10.84 S =  1.22 AGE =   78 H: (not 2)
PV =   542.7935 EPPUB = 0.79 EP = 0.54 N = 10.47 S =  1.41 AGE =    1 H: 1
PV =   531.7935 EPPUB = 0.79 EP = 0.53 N =  2.27 S =  0.00 AGE =    1 H: f
PV =   511.8824 EPPUB = 0.88 EP = 0.51 N =  1.70 S = -4.47 AGE =    5 H: 0
----Level 1----
PV =   544.0000 EPPUB = 1.00 EP = 0.54 N =   0.00 S =  1.41 AGE =    0 H: (sr 1 (not 0) nil)
PV =   534.0000 EPPUB = 1.00 EP = 0.53 N =   0.00 S =  1.41 AGE =    0 H: (sr 1 2 nil)
PV =   532.7935 EPPUB = 0.79 EP = 0.53 N =  0.09 S =  0.00 AGE =    1 H: (and 0 (not 2))
PV =   526.0000 EPPUB = 1.00 EP = 0.53 N =   0.00 S =  0.00 AGE =    0 H: (and 1 (not 2))
*** Reinf = (  51 /   100)  51.00%  Long term = (  51 /   100)  51.00%  ***


******  Tick   200 Summary  ******
----Level 0----
PV =   747.0000 EPPUB = 1.00 EP = 0.75 N =  0.96 S = 10.49 AGE =    0 H: 0
PV =   702.0000 EPPUB = 1.00 EP = 0.70 N =  0.52 S =  0.00 AGE =    0 H: f
PV =   677.6504 EPPUB = 0.65 EP = 0.68 N =  4.90 S = -0.26 AGE =   45 H: (not 1)
PV =   667.0000 EPPUB = 1.00 EP = 0.67 N =  0.26 S = -4.90 AGE =    0 H: 1
PV =   664.6576 EPPUB = 0.66 EP = 0.66 N =  0.00 S = -0.52 AGE =    2 H: t
PV =   639.7690 EPPUB = 0.77 EP = 0.64 N =-10.49 S = -0.96 AGE =   16 H: (not 0)
----Level 1----
PV =   860.9246 EPPUB = 0.92 EP = 0.86 N =  0.63 S = 21.11 AGE =   93 H: (sr 0 1 nil)
PV =   857.8619 EPPUB = 0.86 EP = 0.86 N = -0.04 S =  0.00 AGE =   12 H: (and 0 (not 1))
PV =   845.8794 EPPUB = 0.88 EP = 0.85 N =  0.00 S =  0.21 AGE =    9 H: (sr (not 1) (not 0) t)
PV =   845.0000 EPPUB = 1.00 EP = 0.84 N =  0.00 S =  0.19 AGE =    0 H: (or 0 (not 1))
----Level 0----
PV =   781.7923 EPPUB = 0.79 EP = 0.78 N = 10.49 S =  1.73 AGE =    3 H: (not 0)
PV =   741.0000 EPPUB = 1.00 EP = 0.74 N =  0.00 S =  1.26 AGE =    0 H: t
PV =   714.7400 EPPUB = 0.74 EP = 0.71 N = 17.32 S = 14.14 AGE =  128 H: (not 2)
PV =   709.0000 EPPUB = 1.00 EP = 0.71 N = -4.90 S =  1.05 AGE =    0 H: (not 1)
PV =   664.7935 EPPUB = 0.79 EP = 0.66 N = -1.05 S =  4.90 AGE =    1 H: 1
```

```
PV =     650.7935 EPPUB = 0.79 EP = 0.65 N = -1.26 S =   0.00 AGE =    1 H: f
PV =     625.8824 EPPUB = 0.88 EP = 0.62 N = -1.73 S =-10.49 AGE =    5 H: 0
PV =       1.0000 EPPUB = 1.00 EP = 0.00 N =-14.14 S =-17.32 AGE =    0 H: 2
----Level 1----
PV =     827.9259 EPPUB = 0.93 EP = 0.83 N =  6.93 S =   0.00 AGE =   47 H: (sr 1 0 t)
PV =     712.0000 EPPUB = 1.00 EP = 0.71 N =  0.32 S = 14.43 AGE =    0 H: (sr 1 2 t)
PV =     700.0000 EPPUB = 1.00 EP = 0.70 N = 15.28 S =   0.00 AGE =    0 H: (sr (not 2) (not 1) t)
PV =     695.0000 EPPUB = 1.00 EP = 0.69 N = 14.82 S = -3.32 AGE =    0 H: (sr (not 2) (not 0) t)
*** Reinf = (   84 /   100)   84.00% Long term = ( 135 /   200)   67.50% ***
```

Figure 46

A sample run of the GTRL-S algorithm on the two-bit lights and buttons problem. Only the 4 most predictive hypotheses are shown at each non-atomic level.

8.3.2 Many Lights and Buttons

The lights-and-buttons domain described in section 8.3.1 can be easily extended to have an arbitrary number, M, of lights and buttons. If we let each input bit correspond to a light and each output bit correspond to the pressing of a button, we have an environment with M input and M output bits. The agent is never rewarded for pressing more than one button at once.

The more complex lights-and-buttons problem can be solved by using the CASCADE method in conjunction with GTRL-S, with one copy of the GTRL-S algorithm for each bit of output (corresponding to each button.) Figure 46 shows excerpts from a sample run with two lights and two buttons (this differs from the domain described in the previous section in that there are two output bits rather than only one.) The first two levels belong to the instance of GTRL-S for the first output bit and the second two levels belong to the second instance of GTRL-S. After the first 100 ticks, the second bit has clearly learned to be the negation of the first. We can see this because the prediction age of hypothesis $\neg b_2$ is 78; b_2 here is the output of the first Boolean function learner. The first bit has just constructed its correct hypothesis, $SR(b_0, b_1)$, but has not yet executed it many times. By tick 200, however, the first bit is confirmed in its choice of hypothesis. The second bit has constructed some additional correct hypotheses, including $SR(b_1, b_0)$ and $SR(b_1, b_2)$, and performance is approaching optimal. Again, it is easy to verify that the necessity and sufficiency heuristics are a good guide for the search.

The search heuristics for SR fail us when we wish to extend this problem to a larger number of lights and buttons using a cascade of 3-level instances of GTRL-S. When there are three lights and buttons, the optimal function for the first bit can be most simply expressed as $SR(b_0, b_1 \lor b_2)$. In order to synthesize this expression, the expression

$\neg b_1 \wedge \neg b_2$ must be available at the previous level. For that to happen, $\neg b_1$ and $\neg b_2$ must be highly sufficient, which is false, in general. Thus, the only way to learn this function is to generate all subexpressions exhaustively, which is computationally prohibitive.

8.4 Conclusion

Although the approach embodied in GTRL-S is capable of learning some simple action maps with state, it does not hold much promise for more complex cases. In such cases, it may, in fact, be necessary to learn a state-transition model of the world and values of the world states, using a combination of Rivest and Schapire's [73] method for learning models with hidden state and Sutton's [91] or Whitehead and Ballard's [101] method for "compiling" transition models into action maps. This will be a difficult job—currently available methods for learning models with hidden state only work in deterministic worlds. Even if they did work in nondeterministic worlds, they attempt to model every aspect of the world's state transitions. In realistic environments, there will be many more aspects of the world state than the agent can track, and its choice of which world states to represent must be guided by reinforcement, so that it can learn to make only the "important" distinctions. Drescher's work on generating "synthetic items" [25] is a promising step in this direction. His "schema mechanism" attempts to learn models of the world that will enable problem solving. When it is unsuccessful at discovering which preconditions will cause a particular action to have a particular result, it "reifies" that set of preconditions as an "item" and attempts to discover tests for its truth or falsity. In many cases the reified item turns out to be a particular aspect of the state of the world that is hidden from the agent.

Chapter 9
Delayed Reinforcement

Until now, we have only considered algorithms for learning to act in environments in which local reinforcement is generated each tick, giving the agent all of the information it will ever get about the success or failure of the action it just took. This is a simple instance of the more general case, in which actions taken at a particular time may not be rewarded or punished until some time in the future. This chapter surveys some existing approaches to the problem of learning from delayed reinforcement, focusing on the use of *temporal difference* methods [90], such as Sutton's *adaptive heuristic critic* method [89] and Watkins' *Q-learning* method [98]. It will be shown how these methods can be combined with the pure function-learning algorithms presented in previous chapters to create a variety of systems that can learn from delayed reinforcement.

9.1 Q-Learning

Q-learning is concerned with learning values of $Q(i, a)$, where i is an input, a is an action, and $Q(i, a)$ is the expected discounted reward of taking action a in input state i, then continuing by following the policy of taking the action with the highest Q value. Recalling that $W'(i, a)(i')$ is the probability of ending in state i' given that action a is taken in state i, Q^* can be defined as

$$Q^*(i, a) = er(i, a) + \gamma \sum_{i' \in \mathcal{I}} U^*(i') W'(i, a)(i') ,$$

where

$$U^*(i) = \max_{a \in \mathcal{A}} Q^*(i, a) .$$

The policy of taking the action with the highest Q^* value is unique and optimal.

A traditional way of arriving at values of Q^* would be to learn the probabilistic state transition function W' and the expected reinforcement function er, and then to solve the system of Q^* equations to determine the value of Q^* for every i and a. This method has been used in the dynamic programming community [74], but is not well suited to on-line learning because it requires the problem to be broken down into a learning phase, a compilation phase, and a performance phase. The agent is unable to take advantage of partial information it gathers during the course of learning and is generally not adaptable to changing environments.

Watkins has developed a method for learning Q values that he describes [97] as "incremental dynamic programming by a Monte Carlo method: the agent's experience—the state-transitions and the rewards that the agent observes—are used in place of transition and reward models." The Q-learning algorithm empirically *samples* values of $Q^*(i, a)$, constructing an estimate, $Q(i, a)$, which is equal to the average of

$$r + \gamma U(i_{t+1}),$$

where r is actual the reinforcement gained, i_{t+1} is the actual next state after having taking action a in situation i, and $U(i)$ is defined in the same way as U^*, except with respect to Q. Watkins proved that the Q values will converge to the true Q^* values given, among other conditions, that each input-action pair is experienced an infinite number of times. The Q algorithm is described formally in algorithm 17.

The initial state of the Q algorithm is simply the array of estimated Q values, indexed by the input and action sets. They are typically initialized to 0.

The initial state s_0 is an array indexed by the set of input states and the set of actions, whose elements are initialized to some constant value.

$$u(s, i, a, r) = s[i', a'] = (1 - \alpha)s[i', a'] + \alpha(r' + \gamma U(i))$$

$$e(s, i) = \text{chosen according to the distribution}$$

$$\Pr(a) = \frac{e^{Q(i,a)/T}}{\sum_{a' \in \mathcal{A}} e^{Q(i,a')/T}}$$

where i', a', and r' are the input, action, and reinforcement values from tick $t - 1$, $0 < \alpha < 1$, $0 < \gamma < 1$, and $U(i) = \max_a\{s[i, a]\}$.

Algorithm 17
The Q-learning algorithm

The update function adjusts the estimated Q value of the previous input and action in the direction of

$$r' + \gamma U(i) \ ,$$

which is the actual reinforcement received on the last tick, r', plus a discounted estimate of the value of the current state, $\gamma U(i)$. The function $U(i)$ estimates the value of an input i by returning the estimated Q value of the best action that can be taken from that state. This update rule illustrates the concept of *temporal difference* learning, which was formulated by Sutton [90]. Rather than waiting until a reinforcement value is received and then propagating it back along the path of states that lead up to it, each state is updated as it is encountered by using the discounted estimated value of the next state as a component of the reinforcement. Initially, these estimated values are meaningless, but as the agent experiences the world, they soon begin to converge to the true values of the states.

If the Q values are correct, it is clear that the evaluation function should choose the action a that maximizes $Q(i, a)$ for the current input i. However, this policy does not include any exploration and, if the Q values are not correct, quickly leads to convergence to nonoptimal behavior. Watkins did not suggest a concrete exploration policy, but Sutton [91] has suggested using a stochastic policy which makes use of the Boltzmann distribution. Thus, the evaluation function shown above calculates a probability for executing each action based on its Q value, then draws an action from that distribution. This guarantees that there is always a finite probability that a particular action will be taken, but actions with small Q values will be relatively unlikely to be chosen. The temperature parameter, T, governs the degree of randomness; the higher the value of T the more the distribution is spread out and the more likely an action with a low Q value will be taken.

9.2 *Q-Learning and Interval Estimation*

A more statistically well-founded approach to the problem of exploration in the context of Q learning is to apply the basic idea of interval estimation, choosing the action with the highest upper bound on the underlying Q value. This approach is embodied IEQ, shown in algorithm 18.

This algorithm can use either a normal or nonparametric model to estimate the expected action values. Using the normal distribution as a model can be dangerous, however, because at the beginning of this process, the sample variance is often 0, which causes the confidence intervals to be degenerate. The normal and nonparametric methods for generating confidence intervals were informally discussed in section 4.5.2 and are presented in detail in appendix A.

The function U changes over time, making early reinforcement values no longer representative of the current value of a particular action. This problem is already dealt with, in part, by the nature of the bounded-space nonparametric techniques, because only a sliding window of data is kept and used to generate upper bounds. However, this does not guarantee that poor-looking actions will be taken periodically in order to see if they have improved. One way of doing this is to decay the statistics, periodically dropping old measurements out of the sliding windows, making them smaller. A similar decay process can be used in the normal statistical model, as well. Decaying the statistics will have the effect of increasing upper bounds, eventually forcing the action to be re-executed. This method will keep the algorithm from absolutely converging to the optimal policy, but the optimal policy can be closely approximated by decreasing the decay rate over time. The IEQ algorithm has three parameters: γ, the discount factor, α, the size of the confidence intervals, and δ, the decay rate.

In the context of the Dyna architecture [91], Sutton has recently developed a similar extension to Q-learning, called Dyna-Q+, in which a factor measuring uncertainty about the results of actions is added to the Q values, giving a bonus to exploring actions about which little is known.

9.3 Adaptive Heuristic Critic Method

Sutton [89, 90] has developed a different approach of applying the temporal difference method to learning from delayed reinforcement.

The initial state is an array indexed by the set of input states and the set of actions, whose elements are initial states of a normal or nonparametric central-value estimator.

$$u(s, i, a, r) = \quad s[i', a'] := \text{update-stats}(s[i', a'], r' + \gamma U(i))$$
$$e(s, i) = \quad a \text{ such that } ub_\alpha(s[i, a]) \text{ is maximized}$$

where $0 < \alpha < 1$, $0 \leq \gamma < 1$, and $U(i) = \max_a\{er(s[i, a])\}$ (*er* is an estimate of the expected reinforcement of performing action a in state i).

Algorithm 18
The IEQ algorithm

Rather than learning the value of every action in every input state, the *adaptive heuristic critic* (AHC) method learns an evaluation function that maps input states into their expected discounted future reinforcement values, given that the agent executes the policy it has been executing. One way of viewing this method is that the AHC module is learning to transduce the delayed reinforcement signal into a local reinforcement signal that can be used by any of the algorithms of the previous chapters. The algorithm used to learn from the local reinforcement signal need only optimize the reinforcement received on the next tick; such an algorithm is referred to as a local (as opposed to global) learning algorithm. It is a requirement, however, that the local learning algorithm be capable of learning in nonstationary environments, because the AHC module will be learning a transduction that changes as the agent's policy changes.

The AHC method, in combined operation with an algorithm for learning from local reinforcement, is formally described in algorithm 19. There are two components to the state of the AHC algorithm: the vectors v and c. The v vector contains, at every tick, the current best estimate of the discounted future value of each state with discount rate γ, given that the agent is executing the behavior that it is currently executing. The c vector values represent the "activation" values of the states. States that have been visited recently have high activation values and those that have not been visited recently have low values. Each of these vectors is initialized to contain 0 values.

The initial state, s_0, consists of three parts: two n-dimensional vectors, c and v, and s_l, the initial state of the local learning algorithm.

$$u(s, i, a, r) = \quad \text{for } j := 0 \text{ to } n \text{ do}$$
$$c[j] := \gamma \lambda c[j]$$
$$c[i'] := c[i'] + 1$$
$$vi := v[i]; \quad vi' := v[i']$$
$$\text{for } j := 0 \text{ to } n \text{ do}$$
$$v[j] := v[j] + \alpha c[j] (r' + \gamma vi - vi')$$
$$s_l := u_l(s_l, i'', a'', v[i'])$$
$$e(s, i) = \quad e_l(s_l, i)$$

where i', a', and r' are the input and action values from tick $t - 1$; i'', and a'' are from tick $t - 2$; n is the size of the input set; s_l, u_l and e_l are the internal state, the update function, and the evaluation function of the local learner; $0 \leq \lambda \leq 1$; $0 \leq \gamma < 1$; and $0 \leq \alpha < 1$.

Algorithm 19
The AHC algorithm

The update function first updates the activation values. Each element's activation is multiplied by $\lambda\gamma$, where γ is the discounting rate and λ is an independent factor that controls the degree to which activation is spread backward from the currently active state. Then, the activation of the state whose value is being updated on this tick, state i', is increased by 1. The values of states are adjusted in proportion to their activations, so for $\lambda = 0$, only the currently active state's value is updated on each tick.

Next, the state values in vector v are updated. Each value $v[j]$ is incremented by the product of its activation, $c[j]$, the learning rate, α, and the prediction difference, $r' - \gamma v[i] - v[i']$. The quantity $v[i']$ is the estimated value of state i'. The quantity $r' + \gamma v[i]$ is a one-step lookahead value of state i', computed as the sum of the global value of state i' (as indicated by the reinforcement value r') and the discounted value of the next state, $\gamma v[i]$. Since the one-step lookahead value is a better estimate than the stored value, the difference between the two values can be used as an error signal for updating the stored value. This updating method efficiently propagates global reinforcement values back along the chain of actions that lead to them, making the AHC algorithm another instance of the temporal difference method.

Finally, the update function feeds a learning instance to the update function of the local learning algorithm. The reason for updating the local learner two ticks behind is that if a large reinforcement value is received, we would like it to be reflected in the function learner as soon as possible. However, if a large r is received at time t, it takes two more ticks to receive the data that will allow its effect on v to be calculated. The algorithm would not be incorrect if it performed $s_l := u_l(s_l, i', a', v[i])$ instead, but it would not respond to good or bad results the first time they were encountered.

The AHC algorithm has no effect on the evaluation process and simply calls the evaluation method of the local learning algorithm.

Sutton has shown [90] that, for the nondiscounted case, the expected values of the predictions found by the temporal difference method converge to the ideal predictions if the data sequences are generated by Markov processes and the value of parameter λ equals 0. When $\lambda = 1$, the temporal difference method generates the same weight adjustments as Widrow and Stearns' least mean squares technique [103]. Recently, Dayan [22] has extended Sutton's results to show that the predictions of the temporal difference method, for any value of λ, converge in expected value to the ideal predictions. Of course, when the agent is choosing actions that change the state of the world, the distributions of input instances change and these results do not necessarily hold.

Sutton's presentation of the AHC algorithm was combined with a version of the LARC algorithm for local learning. The AHC method is presented here independent of assumptions about the local learning algorithm. This way of breaking down the problem is very useful, because it allows us to independently choose a local reinforcement-learning algorithm that is appropriate for the sorts of environments in which it will be run for use in combination with the AHC algorithm. In addition, Sutton used linear association methods to store the values of v and c more efficiently. In this version, the activation and state values are simply stored in a table, but it is easy to see how a variety of more efficient (if less precise) associative storage methods could be applied.

There have been a number of implementations of temporal difference algorithms similar to AHC, but none have had a correct analysis of convergence results. The AHC work grew out of the adaptive critic element (ACE) used by Barto, Sutton, and Anderson [12].

Witten's [109] adaptive optimal controller algorithm computes state values as in the AHC algorithm, but differs from Sutton's work in the way it is combined with the local learner. This difference causes its performance to be significantly inferior [89].

One of AI's most striking early successes was Samuel's checkers-playing program [77, 78]. In one of its learning modes, it learned an evaluation function for board positions from reinforcement. Although Samuel's learning procedure is very complex, it can be closely approximated by the AHC algorithm with $\lambda = 1$.

Another, more distantly related, learning method is Holland's bucket brigade method for assigning credit to chains of rules firing in a production system [40]. It differs significantly in the details, but shares the temporal-difference notion of assigning credit along a sequence based on the local predicted improvement rather than waiting for global reinforcement.

9.4 Other Approaches

There have been a number of other approaches to learning from delayed reinforcement. They can be divided into those that learn a world model (generally assuming, unlike Rivest and Schapire [73], that there is no hidden state) and those that do not.

Drescher [25] presents a theory and implementation of learning based on the developmental psychology of Piaget. The agent learns precondition-action-result schemata that allow it to achieve dynamically presented goals. Drescher's methods have been demonstrated in a simple deterministic world with hidden state. There have been a number of other efforts to learn world models. These include the work of Sutton and Pinette [92], Mason, Christiansen, and Mitchell [54], Mel [56], and Shen [85].

There has been a series of attempts to solve the pole-balancing problem using reinforcement. The problem is motivated by a physical system in which a pole is flexibly mounted on a cart. The pole can rotate about its connection to the cart in one dimension, and the cart can move along a one-dimensional track (in the same dimension as the plane in which the pole moves). The goal is to control the cart in such a way as to keep the pole from falling over and to keep the cart from reaching either end of its track. The system is given an encoding of the positions and velocities of the angle of the pole with respect to the cart and the offset of the cart with respect to the midpoint of the track, and the system chooses to apply a fixed-magnitude force on the cart in either a positive or negative direction. Negative reinforcement is received whenever the pole falls over or the cart reaches the end of its track. The system must learn a "bang-bang" control law that maximizes reinforcement by keeping the pole up and the cart within limits for as long as possible.

The first learning solution to this problem was the BOXES system of Michie and Chambers [58]. It was so named because of the quantization of the four-dimensional continuous-valued parameter space into a set of 255 regions or "boxes." Each box was viewed as making a separate decision about whether to generate a "left" or "right" action when the system was in that state, based on the expected run length given each choice of action. Learning only took place after a failure, and each policy was tested for an entire run. The details of the method are complex and somewhat *ad hoc*, but it recognizes the interesting issues of the problem setting, including temporal credit assignment and the tradeoff between acting to gain information and acting to gain reinforcement.

Connell and Utgoff's CART system [21] takes advantage of the continuity of the parameter space, using an algorithm that does not make an *a priori* division of the space into discrete boxes. Points in the state space are determined from experience to be either desirable or not desirable—interpolation is used to determine the desirability of states that have not yet been visited. The system has considerably better performance than either the BOXES system or the application of the AHC algorithm to this problem by Selfridge and Sutton [84] or by Anderson [4, 5]. The difference in performance seems principally to depend on differences in the encodings of the inputs, however.

9.5 Complexity Issues

Whether we are learning action values or an evaluation function, we are confronted again with the problem of high computational complexity.

With the Q and IEQ algorithms, we are back again to the kinds of exponential complexity in the size of the input and output that we have been trying to avoid. Watkins addresses this issue for Q-learning by using Albus' CMAC method [3] for associating Q values with input-action pairs for its "computational speed and simplicity, rather than accuracy or storage economy." It is possible to use a CMAC that is very space efficient, but at a potentially great cost in accuracy.

Another method of improving computational complexity at the expense of accuracy is to use a linear associator to store the values being learned. The Q values could be stored as a function of a bit vector constructed by concatenating the bit-vector encodings of the input state and the action. Sutton uses this method in his implementation of AHC, storing the evaluations of input states as functions of bit-vector encodings of those states.[1] It is difficult to quantify exactly how much expressive power is lost by using such methods and how that loss in expressiveness will impact the performance of the learning methods as a whole. A related method, used by Anderson [4], is to store predictions in a multilayer network trained using the error-backpropagation method (section 3.4.3 describes this method in more detail).

Algorithms, such as IEQ, that must associate a whole collection of data with an input-action pair are harder to make more efficient in this way. Recent work by Chapman and Kaelbling [20] has addressed the problem of using IEQ in large domains by using statistical tests to select salient aspects of the domain to focus on.

9.6 Empirical Comparison

This section describes the results of three different methods of learning from delayed reinforcement in three simple simulated environments.

9.6.1 Environments
The first two environments are taken from Sutton's thesis [89]. Figures 47 and 48 show their state-transition diagrams. The circled numbers are the reinforcement values of the states; most of the states have reinforcement value 0 (which is omitted from the figure). The first

---

[1]It must be remembered that even in cases for which the optimal policy is a low-complexity function of the inputs, the Q function or state evaluation function may be of much higher complexity.

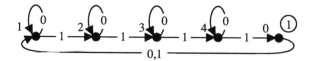

Figure 47
Environment D1: a very simple delayed-reinforcement environment

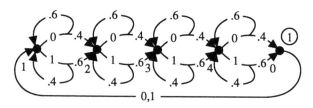

Figure 48
Environment D2: a more difficult delayed-reinforcement environment

is a very easy deterministic environment. The second is a considerably more difficult nondeterministic environment, with little differentiation between "good" and "bad" actions. The third environment, from Watkins [97], is shown in figure 49. It was constructed to be misleading, because, although the correct action in state 0 is 0, if the agent is executing a random policy, the action 1 will have a higher value. Before we apply the learning algorithms to these domains, it is interesting to consider the values of the states and the expected reinforcement of acting optimally in each case.

The optimal strategy for environment D1 is, obviously, always to execute action 1. Because the world is deterministic, it will take five steps to get payoff 1, so the average reinforcement of the optimal policy is 0.2. The values of the states can be calculated by solving the following set of equations, which specify the value of each state in terms of its global value and the discounted value of its successor under the optimal policy:

$$v_0 = 1 + \gamma v_1$$
$$v_1 = \gamma v_2$$
$$v_2 = \gamma v_3$$
$$v_3 = \gamma v_4$$
$$v_4 = \gamma v_0$$

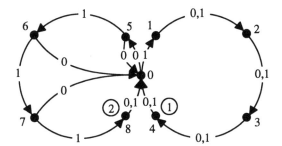

Figure 49
Environment D3: a highly misleading delayed-reinforcement environment

The solution to the equations is

$$v_0 = 1/(1 - \gamma^5)$$
$$v_1 = \gamma^4/(1 - \gamma^5)$$
$$v_2 = \gamma^3/(1 - \gamma^5)$$
$$v_3 = \gamma^2/(1 - \gamma^5)$$
$$v_4 = \gamma/(1 - \gamma^5)$$

which, for $\gamma = .9$, yields the following values: $v_0 = 2.44, v_1 = 1.60, v_2 = 1.78, v_3 = 1.98, v_4 = 2.20$.

The second automaton, D2, is nondeterministic. In this case, the optimal strategy is also always to execute action 1. The expected number of failures preceding the first success in a sequence of Bernoulli trials with probability p is $(1 - p)/p$, so we expect to remain in each of states 1 through 4 for an average of $1 + 0.4/0.6 = 1.67$ steps when executing the optimal policy. Thus, the total expected round-trip time is $4 \times 1.67 + 1 = 6.67$, making the expected reinforcement per tick approximately equal to 0.13. The action values are the solution to the equations

$$v_0 = 1 + \gamma v_1$$
$$v_1 = \gamma(.4v_1 + .6v_2)$$
$$v_2 = \gamma(.4v_2 + .6v_3)$$
$$v_3 = \gamma(.4v_3 + .6v_4)$$
$$v_4 = \gamma(.4v_4 + .6v_0)$$

which, for $\gamma = .9$, is $v_0 = 1.84, v_1 = 0.93, v_2 = 1.10, v_3 = 1.31, v_4 = 1.55$.

Finally, for the complex automaton D3, the optimal strategy is to take action 0 in state 0 and action 1 in states 5, 6 and 7. This path through the transition graph takes 5 steps to gain reinforcement value 2, yielding an average reinforcement per tick of 0.4. The values of the states under the optimal strategy can be expressed as

$$v_0 = \gamma v_5$$
$$v_1 = \gamma v_2$$
$$v_2 = \gamma v_3$$
$$v_3 = \gamma v_4$$
$$v_4 = 1 + \gamma v_0$$
$$v_5 = \gamma v_6$$
$$v_6 = \gamma v_7$$
$$v_7 = \gamma v_8$$
$$v_8 = 2 + \gamma v_0$$

Solving these equations with $\gamma = .9$ yields the state values $v_0 = 3.20, v_1 = 2.83, v_2 = 3.15, v_3 = 3.50, v_4 = 3.88, v_5 = 3.56, v_6 = 3.96, v_7 = 4.40, v_8 = 4.88$.

In order to be sure that we are examining the interesting part of the behavior in each of these environments, runs on environment D1 will be of length 1500; runs on environments D2 and D3 will be of length 5000.

9.6.2 Algorithms
The following three algorithms for learning from delayed reinforcement were tested on each of these problems:

- Q (algorithm 17)
- IEQ (algorithm 18)
- AHC (algorithm 19) in combination with a version of IE (algorithm 10) that uses normal statistics and is modified for use in non-stationary environments.

9.6.3 Parameter Tuning
Each of these algorithms has a number of parameters. Algorithm Q has parameters T, α, and γ; IEQ has parameters α_{ie},[2] γ, and δ; AHC has parameters α, γ, and λ; and IE with normal nonstationary statistics has parameters α_{ie} and δ. The parameter γ is part of the specification

---

[2]Because we are using statistics for the normal distribution, it is easier to express the size of the confidence intervals in terms of α rather than $z_{\alpha/2}$; these are simply two ways of specifying the same parameter.

of the correctness criterion, and it will be set to 0.9 for each algorithm and task.

For each algorithm and environment, a series of 100 trials (length 1500 for D1; length 5000 for D2 and D3) were run with different parameter values. Table 10 shows the best set of parameter values found for each algorithm-environment pair.

9.6.4 Results

Using the best parameter values for each algorithm and environment, the performance of the algorithms was compared on 100 runs of appropriate length. The performance metric was average reinforcement per tick, averaged over the entire run. The results are shown in table 11, together with the expected reinforcement of executing a completely random behavior (choosing actions 0 and 1 with equal probability) and of executing the optimal behavior.

As in the previous sets of experiments, we must examine the relationships of statistically significant dominance among the algorithms for each task. Figure 50 shows, for each task, a pictorial representation of the results of a 1-sided t-test applied to each pair of experimental results. The graphs encode a partial order of significant dominance, with solid lines representing significance at the .95 level.

With the best parameter values for each algorithm, it is also instructive to compare the rate at which performance improves as a function of the number of training instances. Figures 51, 52, and 53 show superimposed plots of the learning curves for each of the algorithms. Each

Table 10
Best parameter values for each algorithm in environments D1, D2, and D3

ALG-TASK	D1	D2	D3
Q			
T	.01	.1	.5
α	.9	.2	.2
IEQ			
α_{ie}	.1	.1	.001
δ	.9999	.999	.99
AHC + IE			
α	.2	.35	.35
λ	.5	.9	1.0
α_{ie}	.01	.01	.001
δ	1	.999	.99

Table 11
Average reinforcement for tasks D1, D2, and D3 over 100 trials

ALG-TASK	D1	D2	D3
Q	.1985	.1182	.3257
IEQ	.1976	.1191	.2462
AHC + IE	.1975	.1251	.2984
random	.1100	.1100	.1250
optimal	.2000	.1300	.4000

point represents the average reinforcement received over a sequence of 100 steps, averaged over 100 runs.

9.6.5 Discussion

There are no clear winners among this set of algorithms. On the simple deterministic task D1, all of the algorithms approach the optimal performance level very closely.

The nondeterministic task D2 is very difficult because of the similarity in transition probabilities between the two actions in each state. On this task, algorithm AHCIE performs very well, with optimal asymptotic performance. The IEQ and Q algorithms perform better than random, but are far from optimal. One conjecture about their poor performance is that, in order for the exploration policies to try each action enough to find the right one, too much exploration takes place. The T parameter for Q is higher and the δ parameter for IEQ is lower than for D1, causing more exploration.

Performance on the difficult problem of task D3 hinges on persistently trying, for a while, courses of action that appear bad. This persistence is necessary to discover that the left loop of the graph is better if the proper action strategy is known. The Q algorithm does a good job of this and comes closer to optimal performance than any of the other

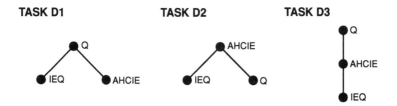

Figure 50
Significant dominance partial order among delayed-reinforcement algorithms for each task

Delayed Reinforcement   137

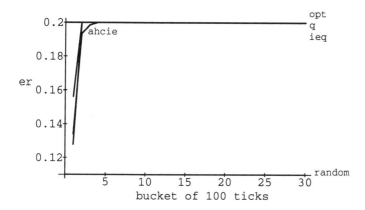

Figure 51
Learning curves for Task D1

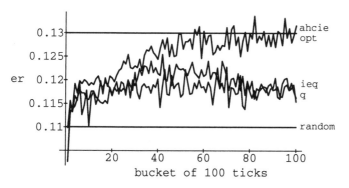

Figure 52
Learning curves for Task D2

algorithms. The other algorithms improve over time, but not nearly as fast. The fact that their performance rises above the .2 level (which is achieved by going around the right loop of the graph) indicates that they are discovering the left loop of the graph. All of the algorithms are parametrized to be very exploratory, which prevents them from asymptotically reaching optimal behavior. In addition, the variance of the performance of IEQ and AHCIE in this domain was quite high; this indicates that the left loop of the graph was found at very different times in different runs.

One important conclusion from these experiments is that the interval-estimation techniques are not very satisfactory in the kinds

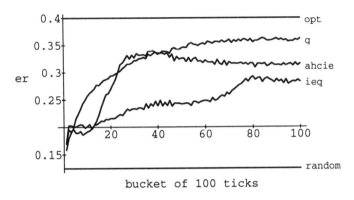

Figure 53
Learning curves for Task D3

of nonstationary environments that are encountered in learning from delayed reinforcement. The initial reinforcement values typically have very low variance, then, as the structure of the world is discovered, they change very quickly. The weight-adjustment techniques seem to handle these changes more flexibly than do the statistical methods tried here. It might be possible to address this by using statistical techniques that, for instance, would notice radically unexpected results or policy changes in one part of the space and make the policy in other parts of the space more highly exploratory in order to take advantage of possible changes. This is an important area for additional research.

Chapter 10

Experiments in Complex Domains

This chapter reports on three experiments comparing algorithms introduced in previous chapters on more complex domains. The first domain is a simulated one with a large number of input and output bits, but with a fairly low-complexity function defining the dependence of each output bit on the input bits. The second domain is a mobile-robot domain in which the agent learns from local reinforcement. The third domain is an extension of the mobile robot domain in which the agent learns from delayed reinforcement. The settings of the experiments will emulate, as much as possible, the deployment of these learning algorithms in realistic domains.

10.1 Simple, Large, Random Environment

This task, in its general form, has M input and M output bits. The optimal action mapping is generated randomly as follows: each output bit is the conjunction or disjunction of two input bits or their negations. If the agent chooses an action in agreement with this mapping, it receives reinforcement value 1 with probability p_1 and 0 otherwise; if the agent's action disagrees with the optimal mapping, it receives reinforcement value 1 with probability p_2 and 0 otherwise.

10.1.1 Algorithms
The following algorithms were tested in this domain:

- IE
- CASCADE + IE
- CASCADE + GTRL

The second and third algorithms consist of a set of Boolean-function learners combined using the CASCADE method. It is expected that the cascade of GTRL algorithms will be both more computationally efficient and learn more quickly than the other three algorithms because the functions are not too complex and the opportunity for generalization is great.

10.1.2 Task

The algorithms were tested on an instance of the general family of large random environments with $M = 8$, $p_1 = .8$, and $p_2 = .1$. It would have been desirable to use an even larger task, but the size of the data structures for the IE and CASCADE + IE algorithms of size $M = 8$ exhausted the available computer memory. Each run of each algorithm was on a newly generated random task with the parameters described above.

10.1.3 Parameter Settings

When we wish to use a learning algorithm in a new setting, we will rarely have the luxury of performing extensive parameter-tuning runs to be sure that we get the best possible performance out of our algorithms. In this experiment, as well as in the other two described in this chapter, parameters for the algorithms will be chosen as well as possible to optimize performance within reasonable complexity constraints based on intuitions gained from the results of previous experiments that we have carried out. There were no test runs used to select parameter values specifically tuned to these problems. The parameter settings were:

IE: $z_{\alpha/2} = 3.0$
CASCADE + IE: $z_{\alpha/2} = 3.0, \delta = .9999$
CASCADE + GTRL: $z_{\alpha/2} = 3.0, \delta = .9999, H = 3M, PA = 20, R = 100$

All of the confidence-interval parameters are set to 3.0 and the decays are .9999. The size of the hypothesis lists, H, in the GTRL algorithm varies linearly as a function of the number of input bits. The number of input instances required for promotion was 20 and new candidates were generated once every 100 ticks.

10.1.4 Results

Each of the algorithms was run for 10 trials of length 10,000 each. This is is a small fraction of the number of trials that would be required for the agent to try all 512 possible actions in each of 512 possible input situations. The average reinforcement for each algorithm on this task is

IE : .1019

CASCADE + IE : .1050

CASCADE + GTRL : .1634

The cascaded generate-and-test algorithm significantly outperforms either of the other algorithms, due to its ability to generalize both over the input and output sets. The learning curves for the algorithms are shown in figure 54. As we can see, the GTRL algorithm improves in performance significantly more quickly than the others. The GTRL algorithm is much more space efficient than the others. It is, theoretically, also more time-efficient as well, but the constant factor is quite large, making it significantly slower than the other methods on this problem. As the size of the input and output spaces grows, however, the GTRL algorithm will become the fastest.

10.2 Mobile Robot Domain

This section describes the application of algorithms from this book to a mobile-robot learning scenario. There have been very few implementations of reinforcement-learning algorithms on real robotic hardware. Three notable examples are: Nehmzow, Smithers and Hallam's [70] work on a reinforcement-like learning problem; Maes and Brooks' [52] use of a simple algorithm to learn to coordinate predefined behaviors on a walking robot; and Mahadevan and Connell's [53] work on learning individual behaviors given a subsumption structure for them.

A number of researchers have applied reinforcement-learning algorithms to simulated robotic domains, such as the cart-pole problem described in chapter 3. Franklin [31] used learning-automata techniques and the A_{RP} algorithm to learn to adjust the outputs of an existing controller to compensate for externally applied torques on a simulated robot arm. In addition, there has been work on learning world models, such as Moore's [66], Miller's [60], and Mel's [56] work on learning a mapping from joint positions to visual coordinates in the workspace of a robotic arm [56] and Mason, Christiansen, and

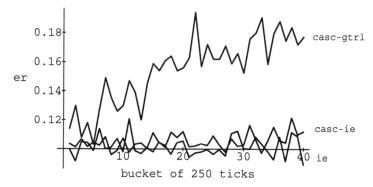

Figure 54
Learning curves for large, random environment

Mitchell's [54] work on learning the results of using a robotic arm to tip a tray of objects in various ways.

The robot pictured in figure 55 was used to validate a variety of reinforcement-learning algorithms. It has two drive wheels, one on each side, which allow it to move forward and backward along circular arcs. A set of five "feelers" allow it to detect obstacles to its front and sides, the round bumper detects contact anywhere on its perimeter, and four photosensors, facing forward, backward, left, and right, measure the light levels in each direction.

10.2.1 Algorithms
The same algorithms and parameter settings were used in this experiment as in the previous one.

10.2.2 Task
In this task, the robot is given negative reinforcement, normally distributed with mean -2.0 and standard deviation 0.5 whenever the round bumper makes contact with any physical object. If the bumper is not engaged, the robot is given positive reinforcement, normally distributed with mean 1.0 and standard deviation 0.2, whenever the light in its front sensor gets brighter. If the bumper has not engaged

Figure 55
Spanky, a mobile robot

and the brightness has not increased, it is given "zero" reinforcement, normally distributed with mean 0.0 and standard deviation 0.2.

The robot interacts with the world by making short fixed-length motions, either forward or rotating in place to the left or right. The agent gets the following five bits of input:

Bits 0 and 1:   Which direction is currently the brightest?
                 00 = front, 01 = left, 10 = right, 11 = back.
Bit 2:   Is the rightmost feeler engaged?
Bit 3:   Is the leftmost feeler engaged?
Bit 4:   Is (at least) one of the middle three feelers engaged?

The agent must learn a mapping from this input space to its three actions that maximizes its local reinforcement. It develops a behavior that avoids bumping into obstacles and tends to move toward the light.

The robot was built using cheap, simple, off-the-shelf components; the aim in its construction was not to have great precision and accuracy. As a result, the sensors and effectors were quite unreliable. A hand-coded strategy that turned away from obstacles and went towards the light, when evaluated according the reinforcement scheme given above, only got an average reinforcement of about 0.4. This was due, in large part, to dramatic fluctuations in the light sensors. Any algorithm that can learn to act reasonably in this domain is doing a good job of locating the signal within the noise.

10.2.3 Results
The robot was run, using the interval estimation algorithm, in this domain for more than 20 trials. It always learned a good local strategy for the domain with the length of time to learn the strategy varying from 2 to 10 minutes depending on how favorable the initial interactions with the world were. These experiments allow us to say, qualitatively, that the learning algorithm worked successfully. We would like, in addition, to compare different learning algorithms quantitatively in this domain.

Ideally, this section would describe a long series of trials of each algorithm on the real mobile robot. Unfortunately, it is difficult to conduct such trials fairly in the physical system. The first problem is that a human must intervene whenever the robot approaches the light source and move the robot to a new location. The second, more difficult, problem is that it takes a long time to conduct the experiments. The time that it takes the robot to move greatly dominates the computation time of the learning algorithms. So, for quantitative experiments with multiple trials, we will make use of an artificial domain. The domain is, superficially, a simulation of the robot domain described above. It is not of high fidelity, which causes this to be a substantially different problem than that of running on the actual robot. Still, it serves as an interesting and slightly complex domain for testing reinforcement-learning algorithms. Also, the results in the simulated domain mirror informal impressions of the relative performance of the algorithms on the actual robot.

In the artificial robot domain, noise is added to the action and perception of the robot. Each action of the simulated robot is, with probability .1, changed to a randomly chosen action; each perception of the state of the world is, with probability .1, changed to a randomly chosen world state. This noise is in no way expected to model the noise occurring in the physical robot domain, which was greater in magnitude and had considerable bias. Whenever the robot reaches the light source in the simulated world, the light is "teleported" to a new randomly chosen location.

The results of running each algorithm for 100 runs of length 2000 are shown in table 12. The optimal expected reinforcement value was estimated by running a hand-crafted nonlearning behavior in the environment under the same conditions as the experimental algorithms. Similarly, the expected reinforcement of a random strategy was estimated by running a random strategy in the world. All of the differences in expected reinforcement are significant. There is only a small difference in performance between the pure IE algorithm and the cascaded version, but the GTRL algorithm performs markedly worse than either of them. As we can see in the learning curves, shown in figure 56, the GTRL algorithm takes longer to converge to its maximum performance, which is lower than optimal because it is continually trying new hypotheses. This problem does not highlight the abilities of the GTRL algorithm, because the input space is fairly small.

Table 12
Average reinforcement for simulated mobile robot environment over 100 runs of length 2000

ALG	er
IE	.6439
CASCADE + IE	.6203
CASCADE + GTRL	.4930
random	.3074
optimal	.6695

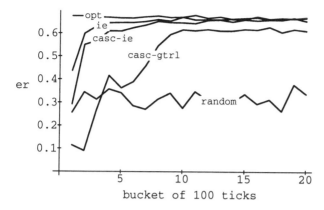

Figure 56
Learning curves for the simulated mobile robot task

10.3 Robot Domain with Delayed Reinforcement

The previous mobile robot domain can be made more difficult by giving the robot a large reinforcement only when it reaches the light source. This problem is considerably more difficult than other domains used in delayed-reinforcement experiments, such as the cart-pole domain. In the cart-pole domain, the robot receives a large negative reinforcement value whenever the pole falls over. In the absence of a good control strategy, the pole will fall over quite readily, giving the learner a lot of useful data early on. In this robot domain, the robot may execute its initial random strategy for a very long time before it accidentally encounters the light source. Informal experiments with the real mobile robot were only successful if a human took an active role near the beginning of the run, putting the robot in situations from which it was relatively easy to reach the light and, therefore, get useful reinforcement data.[1]

This section will report formal experiments carried out in the same simulated robot domain, but with a delayed reinforcement function.

10.3.1 Algorithms

This experiment compares the same algorithms as were compared in the experiment described in section 9.6: Q, IEQ, and AHC + IE. The parameter settings were

---

[1] This process is an instance of a class of methods for expediting learning that are referred to by psychologists [39] as "shaping." Its use in the robot domain described here was suggested by R. Sutton.

Q: $\alpha = .1$, $T = .2$
IEQ: $\alpha_{ie} = .01$, $\delta = .9999$
AHC + IE: $\alpha = .1$, $\lambda = .2$, $\delta = .9999$, $\alpha_{ie} = .05$

10.3.2 Task

The inputs and outputs available to the agent remain the same as in the local reinforcement task. The reinforcement generated by the world is, in this domain, global rather than local. When the agent comes very close to the light source, it is given reinforcement that is normally distributed with mean 10 and standard deviation 2.0; when it bumps into an obstacle, it is given reinforcement normally distributed with mean -2 and standard deviation 0.25; finally, if it neither bumps into the wall nor comes near the light, it is given reinforcement normally distributed with mean 0 and standard deviation 0.25. When the light is reached by the robot, it is randomly moved to a new location.

10.3.3 Results

The results of running each algorithm for 10 runs of length 50,000 are shown in table 13. As before, the optimal expected reinforcement value was estimated by running a hand-crafted nonlearning behavior in the environment under the same conditions as the experimental algorithms. Similarly, the expected reinforcement of a random strategy was estimated by running a random strategy in the world. The performance of Q was significantly better than that of IEQ or AHC + IE, which were not significantly different from one another. The learning curves for this domain are shown in figure 57. The poor performance of the algorithms in this domain may be somewhat deceiving. In many cases, the learning strategies learned quickly to perform at near-optimal levels. However, in many other cases, especially for the IEQ and AHC + IE algorithms, the robot never, or only late in the run, acquired enough experience with the light source to learn an appropriate strategy.

Table 13
Average reinforcement for simulated robot domain with delayed reinforcement over 10 runs of length 50,000

ALG	er
Q	.6529
IEQ	.1468
AHC + IE	.1669
random	−.0927
optimal	1.0591

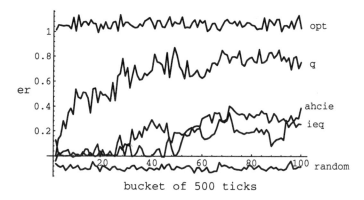

Figure 57
Learning curves for the simulated delayed-reinforcement mobile robot task

For this reason, a "shaping" process used early in the runs would allow the agent to get more useful information and hence improve its performance. An interesting area for future research would be to formally specify such shaping processes and characterize their role in expediting learning.

Chapter 11
Conclusion

This chapter first summarizes the results of the book, then goes on to describe important conclusions that can be drawn from these results. It concludes with a discussion of how the conclusions can direct and inspire future research on building embedded systems that learn from their environments.

11.1 Results

Simple reinforcement-learning problems can be effectively solved using the interval estimation algorithm, which does a good job of making the trade-off between acting to gain reinforcement and acting to gain information. It has two serious limitations, however. First, its computational complexity increases exponentially in the size of the input and output spaces. Second, it exhibits no generalization across input and output instances.

Problems of efficiency and lack of generalization have traditionally been addressed by the use of linear-association and error backpropagation methods for associative reinforcement-learning. Each of these methods has its own problems. The linear-association method can only learn action maps that are in the class of linearly separable functions. Error backpropagation methods can, theoretically, learn functions of arbitrary complexity, but they generally require a large number of presentations of the learning data and are very sensitive to internal parameter values.

In this work, we have pursued the problem of finding new algorithms for efficiently learning limited classes of action maps from reinforcement.

The first step was to simplify the job of the algorithm designer by reducing the problem of learning action maps with many output bits to the problem of learning action maps with a single output bit. The CASCADE method implements this problem reduction, providing decreased time complexity and improved learning rates, as well.

Valiant's algorithm for learning Boolean functions in k-DNF provided a useful foundation for creating new reinforcement-learning algorithms. The LARCKDNF and IEKDNF algorithms integrate the ideas of linear-associative reinforcement comparison and of interval estimation with Valiant's methods. These new algorithms efficiently learn action maps in k-DNF: they are both more time-efficient than the raw IE algorithm, require fewer presentations of data than the BP algorithm, and can learn a larger class of functions than linear-associative approaches.

The GTRL algorithm learns Boolean functions from reinforcement. Its main advantage over the k-DNF methods is that it can learn low-complexity functions very efficiently; however, by changing internal parameter values, it can be configured to learn a variety of different classes of functions with different computational complexities. In addition, its use of internal symbolic representations allows it to be extended to learn simple sequential networks.

All of this work has only addressed the problem of local learning from immediate reinforcement. Existing work on temporal difference methods can also be seen as a problem reduction. It reduces the problem of global learning from delayed reinforcement to the problem of local learning from nonstationary immediate reinforcement. This perspective allows temporal difference methods to be integrated with any available local learning method.

All of these methods can be integrated in various ways, such as using the CASCADE and AHC problem reductions together with the GTRL, LARCKDNF, or IEKDNF algorithms to construct an algorithm that learns an action mapping with many output bits from delayed reinforcement. Many of these methods have been tested and shown to work robustly on a physical mobile robot, demonstrating their applicability to embedded systems in the real world.

11.2 Conclusions

The main conclusion of this work is that it is possible for embedded systems to learn good action strategies from reinforcement in moderately complex, noisy environments. The results are encouraging but also clearly indicate that this learning approach is limited. More specifically, we have observed that

- *It is crucial to have a good exploration strategy.* It is not, in general, difficult to estimate the value of different actions in different situations, but it is difficult to decide which action to take on the basis of their estimated values. The interval estimation method provides a good exploration policy in domains with immediate reinforcement, but does not work particularly well in delayed-reinforcement environments because of nonstationarity.

• *Solving a restricted version of the problem can be very efficient and effective.* There have been good algorithms for quickly solving the subset of learning problems that are linearly separable. The utility of considering restricted versions of a problem is made even more apparent by the results of the algorithms for learning k-DNF and the GTRL algorithm.

• *Learning action maps with state is difficult.* It can be very difficult to notice that there is hidden state in a domain that should be taken into account when choosing actions. In a deterministic domain, it is possible to notice that the same action, when taken in two situations that are nominally the same, has two different results and conclude that there must be some important hidden state. In nondeterministic domains, it is much more difficult to notice such inconsistencies, and a search-based approach foundered due to the lack of good heuristics.

• *Learning from delayed reinforcement is possible, but may require careful design of the domain or of the initial experience.* The algorithms based on temporal-difference methods make effective use of reinforcement data when it is available. In most complex domains, the initial random action policy will execute for a huge amount of time before the system encounters an interesting positive or negative state from which it can learn. We may have to design domains with intermediate "stepping-stones" of reinforcement or take an active role in shaping the agent's behavior.

11.3 Future Work

The initial goal of this work was to build effective embedded systems using whatever techniques were necessary. In the introduction, we saw that direct programming was rarely sufficient due to lack of knowledge on the part of the programmer and lack of flexibility in the resulting system. This book has, so far, considered the opposite case, in which there is as little programming as possible and the system learns a behavior from a *tabula rasa*.

This sort of *tabula rasa* learning clearly has important abilities, as well as limitations, as we have seen. To build truly effective embedded systems, we will have to combine *a priori* knowledge or structure, as provided by a human programmer, with the ability to adapt, as provided by reinforcement-learning algorithms. The remaining sections explore the possibilities for this integration, in the light of the main conclusions of the previous section.

11.3.1 Exploration

If an agent had an *a priori* expectation of how well it needed to perform in the environment, many of the problems of exploration would disappear. Once the agent had found a strategy that worked as well as necessary, it could quit exploring and simply execute the sufficient strategy. In nonstationary environments, the agent would find that, after a while, its previously sufficient policy was no longer sufficient. It would then revert to a more exploratory policy, find a policy sufficient for the newly changed environment, then settle down to executing that policy until the world changed again.

This extension to the current reinforcement-learning paradigm would be very small; the programmer would have to supply a desired average level of reinforcement along with the reinforcement function and would have to be satisfied with any policy that achieved the specified level of reinforcement.

The emphasis on optimality in machine learning has followed a similar emphasis in artificial intelligence and even in computer science in general. In all of these fields there have been discouraging theoretical results about the computational complexity of finding optimal solutions, resulting in a renewed interest in methods that find approximations to the optimal solution or only probably find a good solution. Simon has long advocated "satisficing" or finding solutions that are "good enough" [86]; this sort of approach is finally gaining currency in other areas of artificial intelligence and could be applied very effectively to reinforcement learning.

11.3.2 Bias

The decision to restrict the set of action maps that can be learned can be thought of as the application of a kind of knowledge about the nature of the domain, namely that the optimal or a sufficient action map is within the restricted class. This use of knowledge in machine learning is often called *bias* [65]; bias can restrict the set of possible hypotheses (this case is called *categorical bias*) or put a preference-ordering on them. The stronger the categorical bias, in general, the less data is required to converge to an appropriate hypothesis.

In this work, we have seen a few examples of categorical bias that was based on the form of the action map to be learned. There are many other kinds of bias that are potentially useful and should be explored in the context of reinforcement learning. *Determinations*, introduced by Russell [76], provide an especially useful kind of bias. Determinations are, essentially, descriptions of which input values the outputs depend on. Such information would be of great help in constraining the learning problem when there are large input or output spaces; it could be used to limit the search done by the GTRL algorithm or to limit the set of conjunctive terms in the k-DNF algorithms. This kind of knowledge might also be fairly easy for a human programmer to provide reliably; the programmer must only indicate which perceptual values influence which output values, without specifying the specific nature of the influence.

There are much stronger forms of bias available, as well. The system could be started with a fully specified strategy that was a human programmer's best attempt at a correct program. The system would adopt some sort of exploration policy to see whether improvements could be made, but it would probably be starting from a position of making many of its policy decisions correctly. A useful adjunct to such a learning system would be a programming language that would allow the programmer to specify reactions for different situations and also to specify the level of confidence the programmer has in their correctness. This would allow the system to be more exploratory in situations in which the programmer was less confident.

11.3.3 World Models and State

Learning methods composed of the best techniques described above work effectively in small to medium-sized domains. As the size of domains increases, the effectiveness of the methods tends to degrade. The computational complexity of many of the algorithms is fairly good, so the degradation is not primarily in the space requirements of the methods or the time per learning instance to execute. Rather, it is in the number of learning instances, or interactions with the environment, that the agent must have in order to learn an effective strategy.

One way to learn with fewer interactions with the world is to allow the agent to do some of its experimentation "in its head" rather than directly in the world, by using an internal model of the world. A model of the world consists of two parts: a description of the state-transition function (can be deterministic or not), which maps states and actions into new states, and a description of the reinforcement function, which maps states into reinforcement values. An agent with such an internal world model can, in Popper's words (according to Dennett) [23] "permit its hypotheses to die in its stead," by trying out different courses of action through mental simulation, using the state-transition and reinforcement models. Although this may take some computation time, reinforcement penalties do not accrue for doing the wrong thing. Having a partial world model will also allow an agent to learn the rest of the world model more effectively, by allowing it to experiment in a more informed way. If there is a part of its space the agent does not yet have very much experience with, it can use its existing world model to "plan" a course of action to get to that part of the space much sooner than it would if it had to stumble upon it through random exploration. This is an extension of the exploration versus exploitation trade-off that was discussed above.

Sutton [91] and Whitehead and Ballard [101], among others, have advocated this approach in the context of reinforcement learning. In situations where a correct world model is given in advance, results are very encouraging. However, that is a rather unreasonable scenario; if we had a complete and correct world model initially, we could simply calculate the optimal policy and be done. The more reasonable scenario is one in which the model is learned during the agent's interaction with the world. Empirical studies of such a scenario [50] have not yet clearly shown that it helps to learn a world model. The difficulty is that, initially, the world model is of no help because it is incorrect. By the time the agent has acquired a fairly correct world model, it could also have learned a good policy by standard policy-learning methods.

Improving Model Learning   There are many representational weaknesses in the model-learning approach as it has been implemented. All of the existing work using world models has assumed a deterministic environment, allowing the state-transition model to consist of a mapping from initial states and actions into resulting states, and the reinforcement model to be a mapping from states to scalar values. In a nondeterministic domain, a state-transition model of the environment must consist of a mapping from initial states and actions into a probability distribution over resulting states. Similarly, the reinforcement model must map states into distributions over reinforcement values (or, at least, the centers of the distributions). If such a mapping could be learned, then either the optimal policy could be calculated from it using dynamic programming methods, or it could be used incrementally, in the style of Dyna [91], to simulate learning steps in the environment.

Learning such models for anything but a very small domain is a nearly hopeless task, however. The size grows quickly in increased size of input and output spaces, and the model suffers from problems of compartmentalization of information. This problem can be ameliorated by applying standard function-approximation techniques to decrease space requirements and to increase generalization across similar situations and actions.

Function-approximation techniques are general-purpose; they will learn the same approximation of the world model no matter what the agent's goals (or reinforcement function) are. It would make more sense for the the kinds of approximations the agent makes in modeling the world to depend on the kinds of tasks it is trying to accomplish. If the agent's only goals concern navigation, it may not be at all important to store information about color change in the environment (on the other hand, if colors serve as important navigational cues, then it may).

Another thing to notice is that the current world models consist of a description of how entire states are mapped to other entire states under particular actions. The AI planning community has done a great deal of work on describing state-transition models of worlds (although they are usually deterministic), but they rarely, if ever, consider describing the mapping at this level. Rather, they take advantage of the compositional structure of the domain, noticing that states that have a certain *property* tend to be mapped to states that have a certain other *property* under a particular action. Such structure allows them to describe the world in terms of operator descriptions, which specify what must be true in the world given that certain conditions held initially and a particular action was taken. Given a compositional transition model of the world, a particular fully specified state can be mapped into another fully specified state, but the mapping can be represented much more compactly and will, as a side effect, tend to make appropriate generalizations by ignoring those properties of the initial state that are irrelevant to the result. There are domains for which no such compositional model can be obtained; in these domains, every aspect of the outcome of a particular action depends on every aspect of the situation in which that action was taken, and learning will be intractable no matter what approach is taken.

An important research direction is to develop methods for learning approximate world models in nondeterministic reinforcement-learning problems. The models should have the property that the details of the approximation depend on the task of the agent and should exploit the compositional structure of the environment.

Using Approximate World Models   Approximate world models, in the form of probabilistic operator descriptions, can be used to simulate interactions with the world and, thereby, to construct a policy for acting in the world. Following the Dyna method [91], the agent will update its policy both by taking steps in the real world (information gained from these steps can be used to update the model) and by taking imagined steps in the internal model.

In the simplest way of using the model to simulate results, the agent decides to consider what would happen if it were to take a particular action in a particular situation. It applies any operator descriptions that are appropriate to the action and whose preconditions are satisfied in that situation; from these it generates a distribution on possible resulting situations. It draws from the distribution to get a resulting situation, then evaluates the reinforcement model on that situation. It now has a situation, action, result triple which it can use as data for conventional reinforcement-learning methods.

In order to control exploration, the agent must notice that there is a certain state or class of states that it has very little experience with. It may then do something very similar to classical backward planning, looking in its repertoire of operator descriptions for one that has the little-experienced condition as one of its likely results. It can then back-chain until it finds a sequence of actions that is likely to reach the little-known state from the current one. It will execute the first of those actions, then repeat the planning-for-exploration process.

One of the important difficulties of past work that uses a learned world model is that while the model is first being learned, its use is detrimental to the process of policy formation. An improvement would be only to use the model when its predictions are fairly accurate. Since the probabilistic operator descriptions we are proposing to learn are based directly on statistical evidence, it will be possible to construct a measure of reliability of operator descriptions and to use their predictions only when the reliability exceeds a certain threshold.

Learning Models with Hidden State   It is rarely the case that an agent can instantaneously perceive all of the relevant state of the world. In order to be able to discriminate the state of the world more finely, and hence to act more appropriately, the agent must be able to track certain aspects of the world that are not directly perceivable. Of course, there will be infinitely many such aspects, so it will again be necessary to apply task-driven techniques to choose to track only those aspects that enable the agent to perform more appropriately given its reinforcement function.

How can we know if there is hidden state in a nondeterministic world? The answer is probably that we cannot. However, if we assume that the environments we are dealing with have certain useful properties of predictability, it may be appropriate to postulate the existence of hidden state when it is not possible to find a low-entropy operator description for certain salient postconditions. It may be that whenever an especially good state, s, is reached, it is reached by performing action a. However, performing action a seems to have many other possible results, as well. When we try to construct an operator description concerning action a with s as one of the postconditions, we find that there are no preconditions that make s (or anything else) a very likely outcome. We may postulate that some hidden condition must obtain for action *a* to lead to state *s*.

11.3.4 Delayed Reinforcement

In learning from delayed reinforcement, we have to ensure that interesting good and bad results will happen to the system so it has an opportunity to learn. In situations like the robot domain studied in chapter 10, there is a real problem that the initial random strategy of the system would run for a very long time before an interesting reinforcement even happened. We briefly discussed shaping as an appropriate kind of help in such situations: a teacher starts the system initially in configurations from which it is easy to reach an interesting result; as the system learns to deal with these situations, it is moved to progressively more difficult situations.

Another way to make learning from delayed reinforcement more effective is to supply a teacher. Of course, if the system gets to observe the teacher perfectly, our problem is reduced to simple supervised learning. A weaker teacher might supply only a few interesting trajectories through the space and leave the system to explore their connections and alternate paths. Some scenarios of this kind have been studied by Whitehead [100] and by Lin [50].

Learning from delayed reinforcement can also benefit significantly from initial strategies that are supplied by a programmer. As in most problems of computer science, learning in complex systems can be made much more efficient by breaking a large problem into a number of smaller problems. In general, there may not be a domain-independent way of doing this, although there are interesting results along this line by Singh [87]. An alternative is for the programmer to specify a break-down of the task into subtasks; this was done by Mahadevan and Connell [53] in a way that required the programmer to specify separate reinforcement functions for each submodule. It will take further experimentation to see if this is an appropriate division of labor between man and machine.

11.4 Final Words

This work represents some steps toward the final goal of the synthesis of complex embedded systems through a combination of *a priori* design and on-line learning. There is still a long way to go down this path, but it is hoped that these steps will provide a sound start.

Appendix A

Statistics in GTRL

A.1 Binomial Statistics

Each hypothesis has the following set of statistics associated with it:

b_{0s} The number of times action 0 was taken when this hypothesis was satisfied and reinforcement value 0 was received (mnemonically "bad 0 satisfied").

b_{0n} The number of times action 0 was taken when this hypothesis was not satisfied and reinforcement value 0 was received (mnemonically "bad 0 not-satisfied").

b_{1s} The number of times action 1 was taken when this hypothesis was satisfied and reinforcement value 0 was received (mnemonically "bad 1 satisfied").

b_{1n} The number of times action 1 was taken when this hypothesis was not satisfied and reinforcement value 0 was received (mnemonically "bad 1 not-satisfied").

g_{0s} The number of times action 0 was taken when this hypothesis was satisfied and reinforcement value 1 was received (mnemonically "good 0 satisfied").

g_{0n} The number of times action 0 was taken when this hypothesis was not satisfied and reinforcement value 1 was received (mnemonically "good 0 not-satisfied").

g_{1s} The number of times action 1 was taken when this hypothesis was satisfied and reinforcement value 1 was received (mnemonically "good 1 satisfied").

g_{1n} The number of times action 1 was taken when this hypothesis was not satisfied and reinforcement value 1 was received (mnemonically, "good 1 not-satisfied").

pb_0 The number of times this hypothesis has chosen the action 0 and received reinforcement value 0 (mnemonically, "predicted bad 0").

pb_1 The number of times this hypothesis has chosen the action 1 and received reinforcement value 0.

pg_0 The number of times this hypothesis has chosen the action 0 and received reinforcement value 1 (mnemonically, "predicted good 0").

pg_1 The number of times this hypothesis has chosen the action 1 and received reinforcement value 1.

The procedure for updating these statistics should be apparent from the descriptions given above.

Most of the statistics are concerned with what happens when the hypothesis agreed with the action that was actually taken; this will be the case when the action was 1 and the hypothesis was satisfied and when the action was 0 and the hypothesis was not satisfied. Given this data structure, we can define the statistical functions as follows:

$$age(h) = b_{0n} + b_{1s} + g_{0n} + g_{1s}$$

$$er(h) = \frac{g_{0n} + g_{1s}}{b_{0n} + b_{1s} + g_{0n} + g_{1s}}$$

$$er\text{-}ub(h) = ub(g_{0n} + g_{1s}, b_{0n} + b_{1s} + g_{0n} + g_{1s})$$

$$erp(h) = \frac{pg_0 + pg_1}{pb_0 + pb_1 + pg_0 + pg_1}$$

$$erp\text{-}ub(h) = ub(pg_0 + pg_1, pb_0 + pb_1 + pg_0 + pg_1)$$

$$N(h) = Z(g_{0n}, g_{0n} + b_{0n}, g_{1n}, g_{1n} + b_{1n})$$

$$S(h) = Z(g_{1s}, g_{1s} + b_{1s}, g_{0s}, g_{0s} + b_{0s})$$

where the upper-bound function, ub, is defined [48] as

$$ub(x, n) = \frac{\frac{x}{n} + \frac{z_{\alpha/2}^2}{2n} + \frac{z_{\alpha/2}}{\sqrt{n}}\sqrt{\left(\frac{x}{n}\right)\left(1 - \frac{x}{n}\right) + \frac{z_{\alpha/2}^2}{4n}}}{1 + \frac{z_{\alpha/2}^2}{n}} ,$$

and the Z function is the normal deviate returned by the standard binomial test for difference of parameter, given by [88]:

$$Z(s_1, n_1, s_2, n_2) = \frac{p_1 - p_2}{\sqrt{\frac{p_1(1-p_1)}{n_1} + \frac{p_2(1-p_2)}{n_2}}} ,$$

where $p_1 = s_1/n_1$ and $p_2 = s_2/n_2$. The parameter $z_{\alpha/2}$ is used to determine the size of the confidence interval for computing ub.

A.2   Normal Statistics

Each hypothesis has the following set of statistics associated with it:

n_{0s} The number of times action 0 has been taken when this hypothesis was satisfied.

s_{0s} The sum of reinforcement values received when action 0 was taken when this hypothesis was satisfied.

ss_{0s} The sum of the squares of the reinforcement values received when action 0 was taken when this hypothesis was satisfied.

n_{0n} The number of times action 0 has been taken when this hypothesis was not satisfied.

s_{0n} The sum of reinforcement values received when action 0 was taken when this hypothesis was not satisfied.

ss_{0n} The sum of the squares of the reinforcement values received when action 0 was taken when this hypothesis was not satisfied.

n_{1s} The number of times action 1 has been taken when this hypothesis was satisfied.

s_{1s} The sum of reinforcement values received when action 1 was taken when this hypothesis was satisfied.

ss_{1s} The sum of the squares of the reinforcement values received when action 1 was taken when this hypothesis was satisfied.

n_{1n} The number of times action 1 has been taken when this hypothesis was not satisfied.

s_{1n} The sum of reinforcement values received when action 1 was taken when this hypothesis was not satisfied.

ss_{1n} The sum of the squares of the reinforcement values received when action 1 was taken when this hypothesis was not satisfied.

n_p The number of times this hypothesis has chosen an action.

s_p The sum of reinforcement values received when the hypothesis has chosen an action.

ss_p The sum of the squares of the reinforcement values received when the hypothesis has chosen an action.

The procedure for updating these statistics should be apparent from the descriptions given above.

As in the binomial case, most of the statistics are concerned with what happens when the hypothesis agreed with the action that was actually taken; this will be the case when the action was 1 and the hypothesis was satisfied and when the action was 0 and the hypothesis was not satisfied. Given this data structure, we can define the statistical functions as follows:

$$age(h) = n_{0n} + n_{1s}$$

$$er(h) = \frac{s_{0n} + s_{1s}}{n_{0n} + n_{1s}}$$

$$er\text{-}ub(h) = nub(n_{0n} + n_{1s}, s_{0n} + s_{1s}, ss_{0n} + ss_{1s})$$

$$erp(h) = \frac{s_p}{n_p}$$

$$er\text{-}ub(h) = nub(n_p, s_p, ss_p)$$

$$N(h) = T(n_{0n}, s_{0n}, ss_{0n}, n_{1n}, s_{1n}, ss_{1n})$$

$$S(h) = T(n_{1s}, s_{1s}, ss_{1s}, n_{0s}, s_{0s}, ss_{0s})$$

where the normal upper-bound function, nub, is defined as

$$nub(n, \sum x, \sum x^2) = \bar{x} + t_{\alpha/2}^{(n-1)} \frac{\sigma}{\sqrt{n}}$$

where $\bar{x} = x/n$ is the sample mean,

$$\sigma = \sqrt{\frac{n \sum x^2 - (\sum x)^2}{n(n-1)}}$$

is the sample standard deviation, $t_{\alpha/2}^{(n)}$ is Student's t function with $n-1$ degrees of freedom [88]. The function T is the result of a test for equal means, not assuming equal variances; it is not distributed exactly as Student's t, but can be approximated using that distribution [88]; it is defined as

$$T(n_1, \sum x_1 \sum x_1^2, n_2, \sum x_2, \sum x_2^2) = \frac{\bar{x}_1 - \bar{x}_2}{\sqrt{\frac{s_1^2}{n_1} + \frac{s_2^2}{n_2}}},$$

where x_1 and x_2 are sample means and s_1 and s_2 are sample standard deviations as defined above. The parameter $z_{\alpha/2}$ is used to determine the size of the confidence interval for computing nub.

A.3 Nonparametric Statistics

This statistical module is parametrized by w, the window size, as well as by the confidence-interval parameter $z_{\alpha/2}$. The parameter w controls the size of the data buffers kept by the module. Because this method employs no summary statistics, all of the data for the last w ticks are stored in this module. Each hypothesis has the following set of statistics associated with it:

n The number of times this hypothesis has agreed with the action taken.

r_t A list of the reinforcement values of the last w ticks on which this hypothesis agreed with the action taken, sorted increasing by time received.

r_v A list of the reinforcement values of the last w ticks on which this hypothesis agreed with the action taken, sorted increasing by value.

n_0 The number of times this hypothesis has agreed with the action 0.

r_{t0} A list of the reinforcement values of the last w ticks on which this hypothesis agreed with the action 0, sorted increasing by time received.

r_{v0} A list of the reinforcement values of the last w ticks on which this hypothesis agreed with the action 0, sorted increasing by value.

n_1 The number of times this hypothesis has agreed with the action 1.

r_{t1} A list of the reinforcement values of the last w ticks on which this hypothesis agreed with the action 1, sorted increasing by time received.

r_{v1} A list of the reinforcement values of the last w ticks on which this hypothesis agreed with the action 1, sorted increasing by value.

n_p The number of times this hypothesis has chosen the action.

r_{tp} A list of the reinforcement values of the last w ticks on which this hypothesis chose the action, sorted increasing by time received.

r_{vp} A list of the reinforcement values of the last w ticks on which this hypothesis chose the action, sorted increasing by value.

Updating these statistics is slightly more complex that in the previous cases. The n's are simply incremented appropriately. As long as the n value is less than or equal to w, new data are simply inserted into the appropriate places in the lists. Once n is greater than w, on each tick, the first element of r_t is removed from both r_t and r_v, and the new reinforcement value is inserted into the resulting r_v and put on the end of the resulting r_t. This keeps the window of data sliding along. We need r_t in order to know which element to remove from r_v before we can add a new element.

Given this data structure, we can define the statistical functions, using the ordinary sign test [33], as follows:

$$age(h) = n$$
$$er(h) = r_v[\lfloor \min(w, n)/2 \rfloor]$$

$$er\text{-}ub(h) = r_v[\min(w, n) - u]$$
$$erp(h) = r_{vp}[\lfloor \min(w, n_p)/2 \rfloor]$$
$$er\text{-}ub(h) = r_{vp}[\min(w, n_p) - u]$$

where value u is chosen to be the largest value such that

$$\left(\begin{array}{c} \sum_{k=0}^{u} \\ nk.5^n \leq \alpha/2 \end{array} \right) .$$

For large values of n, u can be approximated using the normal distribution.

The computation of N and S can be done using a two-sample Kolmogorov-Smirnov test or a median test; these tests are too complex to describe here, but are covered in detail by Gibbons [33].

Appendix B

Simplifying Boolean Expressions in GTRL

This appendix describes the Boolean canonicalization and simplification rules that are used in the GTRL algorithm. It is assumed that simplification happens when a conjunction, disjunction, or set-reset expression is being constructed and that the arguments have already been simplified and canonicalized. The algorithm is described as first constructing the combined hypothesis, then testing to see if has depth appropriate to the level of the algorithm for which it was constructed. In fact, the procedures for constructing composite hypotheses simply return nil if any applicable simplification rules can be found.

The disjunctive hypothesis $e_1 \lor e_2$ can be simplified to a lower level of complexity if any of the following statements is true (e stands for any expression):

$e_1 = e_2$

$e_1 = \textbf{false}$

$e_1 = \textbf{true}$

$e_2 = \textbf{false}$

$e_2 = \textbf{true}$

$e_1 = \neg e_2$

$e_2 = \neg e_1$

$e_1 = e_2 \lor e$

$e_1 = e \lor e_2$

$e_2 = e_1 \lor e$

$e_2 = e \lor e_1$

$e_1 = e_2 \land e$

$e_1 = e \land e_2$

$e_2 = e_1 \land e$

$e_2 = e \land e_1$

The conjunctive hypothesis $e_1 \wedge e_2$ can also be simplified in any of the situations described above. The set-reset hypothesis $SR(e_1, e_2)$ can be simplified in all of the situations described above, except the ones in which $e_1 = e_2 \wedge e$ or $e_1 = e \wedge e_2$. To see this, note that $SR(a, a \wedge b) = SR(a, b)$ because setting takes priority, but $SR(a \wedge b, a)$ cannot be reduced.

Canonicalization consists of ordering the two top-level subexpressions, because they are assumed to have already been canonicalized. An arbitrary ordering is defined on operators; atomic expressions referring to input bits are ordered according to their index into the input vector. The expression e_1 is less than expression e_2 if and only if

- e_1 and e_2 are both atoms and $e_1 < e_2$;
- e_1 is an atom and e_2 is not;
- neither e_1 nor e_2 is an atom and the top level operator of e_1 is less than the top level operator of e_2;
- neither e_1 nor e_2 is an atom, they both have the same top-level operator, and the first subexpression of e_1 is less than (under this definition) the first subexpression of e_2; or
- neither e_1 nor e_2 is an atom, they both have the same top-level operator, they both have the same first subexpression, and the second subexpression of e_1 is less than (under this definition) the second subexpression of e_2.

References

[1] Philip E. Agre and David Chapman. Pengi: An implementation of a theory of activity. In *Proceedings of the Sixth National Conference on Artificial Intelligence*, volume 1, pages 268–272, Seattle, Washington, 1987. Morgan Kaufmann.

[2] David W. Aha and Dennis Kibler. Noise tolerant instance-based learning algorithms. In *Proceedings of the Eleventh International Joint Conference on Artificial Intelligence*, volume 1, pages 794–799, Detroit, Michigan, 1989. Morgan Kaufmann.

[3] James S. Albus. *Brains, Behavior, and Robotics*. BYTE Books, Subsidiary of McGraw-Hill, Peterborough, New Hampshire, 1981.

[4] Charles W. Anderson. *Learning and Problem Solving with Multilayer Connectionist Systems*. PhD thesis, University of Massachusetts, Amherst, Massachusetts, 1986.

[5] Charles W. Anderson. Strategy learning with multilayer connectionist representations. In *Proceedings of the Fourth International Workshop on Machine Learning*, pages 103–114, Ann Arbor, Michigan, 1987.

[6] Dana Angluin and Philip Laird. Learning from noisy examples. *Machine Learning*, 2(4):343–370, 1988.

[7] W. Ross Ashby. *Design for a Brain: The Origin of Adaptive Behaviour*. John Wiley and Sons, New York, New York, second edition, 1960.

[8] A. G. Barto and P. Anandan. Pattern recognizing stochastic learning automata. *IEEE Transactions on Systems, Man, and Cybernetics*, 15:360–374, 1985.

[9] A. G. Barto, R. S. Sutton, and C. J. C. H. Watkins. Learning and sequential decision making. Technical Report 89-95, Department of Computer and Information Science, University of Massachusetts, Amherst, Massachusetts, 1989. Also published in *Learning and Computational Neuroscience: Foundations of Adaptive Networks*, Michael Gabriel and John Moore, editors. The MIT Press, Cambridge, Massachusetts, 1991.

[10] Andrew G. Barto. Connectionist learning for control. Technical Report 89-89, Department of Computer and Information Science, University of Massachusetts, Amherst, Massachusetts, 1989.

[11] Andrew G. Barto and Michael I. Jordan. Gradient following without back-propagation in layered networks. In *Proceedings of the IEEE First*

International Conference on Neural Networks, volume 2, pages 629–636, San Diego, California, 1987.

[12] Andrew G. Barto, Richard S. Sutton, and Charles W. Anderson. Neuronlike adaptive elements that can solve difficult learning control problems. *IEEE Transactions on Systems, Man, and Cybernetics*, SMC-13(5):834–846, 1983.

[13] Donald A. Berry and Bert Fristedt. *Bandit Problems: Sequential Allocation of Experiments*. Chapman and Hall, London, 1985.

[14] L. Blum and N. Blum. Towards a mathematical theory of inductive inference. *Information and Control*, 28:125–155, 1975.

[15] Rodney A. Brooks. A robust layered control system for a mobile robot. *IEEE Journal of Robotics and Automation*, RA-2:14–23, 1986.

[16] Rodney A. Brooks, Anita M. Flynn, and Thomas Marill. Self calibration of motion and stereo vision for mobile robot navigation. Technical Report AIM-984, MIT Artificial Intelligence Laboratory, Cambridge, Massachusetts, 1987.

[17] Wray Buntine. A critique of the Valiant model. In *Proceedings of the Eleventh International Joint Conference on Artificial Intelligence*, volume 1, pages 837–842, Detroit, Michigan, 1989. Morgan Kaufmann.

[18] Robert R. Bush and William K. Estes, editors. *Studies in Mathematical Learning Theory*. Stanford University Press, Stanford, California, 1959.

[19] David Chapman. Planning for conjunctive goals. *Artificial Intelligence*, 32(3):333–378, 1987.

[20] David Chapman and Leslie Pack Kaelbling. Input generalization in delayed reinforcement learning: An algorithm and performance comparisons. In *Proceedings of the International Joint Conference on Artificial Intelligence*, Sydney, Australia, 1991.

[21] Margaret E. Connell and Paul E. Utgoff. Learning to control a dynamic physical system. In *Proceedings of the Sixth National Conference on Artificial Intelligence*, volume 2, pages 456–460, Seattle, Washington, 1987. Morgan Kaufmann.

[22] Peter Dayan. The convergence of TD(λ) for general λ. *Machine Learning*, 8(3):341–362, 1992.

[23] Daniel C. Dennett. *Brainstorms: Philosophical Essays on Mind and Psychology*. Bradford Books, Montgomery, Vermont, 1978.

[24] Thomas G. Dietterich. Learning at the knowledge level. *Machine Learning*, 1(3):287–315, 1986.

[25] Gary L. Drescher. *Made-up Minds: A Constructivist Approach to Artificial Intelligence*. The MIT Press, Cambridge, Massachusetts, 1991.

[26] Richard O. Duda, John Gaschnig, and Peter E. Hart. Model design in the Prospector consultant system for mineral exploration. In Donald Michie, editor, *Expert Systems in the Micro Electronic Age*. Edinburgh University Press, Edinburgh, U.K., 1979.

[27] Richard O. Duda, Peter E. Hart, and Nils J. Nilsson. Subjective Bayesian methods for rule-based inference systems. Technical Report 124, Artificial Intelligence Center, SRI International, Menlo Park, California, 1976.

[28] Herbert B. Enderton. *A Mathematical Introduction to Logic*. Academic Press, New York, New York, 1972.

[29] William K. Estes. Toward a statistical theory of learning. *Psychological Review*, 57:94–107, 1950.

[30] R. James Firby. An investigation into reactive planning in complex domains. In *Proceedings of the Sixth National Conference on Artificial Intelligence*, volume 1, pages 202–206, Seattle, Washington, 1987. Morgan Kaufmann.

[31] Judy A. Franklin. Learning control in a robotic system. In *Proceedings of the IEEE International Conference on Systems, Man, and Cybernetics*, 1987.

[32] King-Sun Fu. Learning control systems—review and outlook. *IEEE Transactions on Automatic Control*, 15(2):210–221, April 1970.

[33] Jean Dickinson Gibbons. *Nonparametric Statistical Inference*. Marcel Dekker, Inc., New York and Basel, 1985.

[34] E. Mark Gold. Language identification in the limit. *Information and Control*, 10:447–474, 1967.

[35] E. Mark Gold. Complexity of automaton identification from given data. *Information and Control*, 37:302–320, 1978.

[36] David E. Goldberg. *Genetic Algorithms in Search, Optimization, and Machine Learning*. Addison-Wesley, Reading, Massachusetts, 1989.

[37] John J. Grefenstette. Incremental learning of control strategies with genetic algorithms. In *Proceedings of the Sixth International Workshop on Machine Learning*, pages 340–344, Ithaca, New York, 1989. Morgan Kaufmann.

[38] David Haussler. Quantifying inductive bias: AI learning algorithms and Valiant's learning framework. *Artificial Intelligence*, 36(2):177–222, 1988.

[39] Ernest R. Hilgard and Gordon H. Bower. *Theories of Learning*. Prentice-Hall, Englewood Cliffs, New Jersey, fourth edition, 1975.

[40] John H. Holland. Escaping brittleness: The possibilities of general-purpose learning algorithms applied to parallel rule-based systems. In Ryszard S. Michalski, Jaime G. Carbonell, and Tom M. Mitchell, editors, *Machine Learning: An Artificial Intelligence Approach*, volume 2, chapter 20. Morgan Kaufmann, 1986.

[41] Leslie Pack Kaelbling. Learning as an increase in knowledge. Technical report, Center for the Study of Language and Information, Stanford, California, 1987.

[42] Leslie Pack Kaelbling. Goals as parallel program specifications. In *Proceedings of the Seventh National Conference on Artificial Intelligence*, Minneapolis-St. Paul, Minnesota, 1988.

[43] Leslie Pack Kaelbling. *Learning in Embedded Systems*. PhD thesis, Stanford University, Stanford, California, 1990.

[44] Leslie Pack Kaelbling. Compiling operator descriptions into reactive strategies using goal regression. Technical report, Teleos Research, Palo Alto, California, 1991.

[45] Leslie Pack Kaelbling and Stanley J. Rosenschein. Action and planning in embedded agents. *Robotics and Autonomous Systems*, 6(1):35–48, 1990. Also published in *Designing Autonomous Agents: Theory and Practice from Biology to Engineering and Back*, Pattie Maes, editor, The MIT Press/Elsevier, 1991.

[46] John G. Kemeny and J. Laurie Snell. *Finite Markov Chains*. Springer-Verlag, New York, 1976.

[47] Tze Leung Lai. Adaptive treatment allocation and the multi-armed bandit problem. *The Annals of Statistics*, 15(3):1091–1114, 1987.

[48] Richard J. Larsen and Morris L. Marx. *An Introduction to Mathematical Statistics and Its Applications*. Prentice-Hall, Englewood Cliffs, New Jersey, 1986.

[49] Long-Ji Lin. Self-improving based on reinforcement learning, planning, and teaching. In *Proceedings of the Eighth International Workshop on Machine Learning*, Evanston, Illinois, 1991. Morgan Kaufmann.

[50] Long-Ji Lin. Self-improving reactive agents based on reinforcement learning, planning and teaching. *Machine Learning*, 8(3):293–322, 1992.

[51] Nick Littlestone. Learning quickly when irrelevant attributes abound: A new linear threshold algorithm. *Machine Learning*, 2(4):245–318, 1988.

[52] Pattie Maes and Rodney A. Brooks. Learning to coordinate behaviors. In *Proceedings of the Eighth National Conference on Artificial Intelligence*, Boston, Massachusetts, 1990. Morgan Kaufmann.

[53] Sridhar Mahadevan and Jonathan Connell. Automatic programming of behavior-based robots using reinforcement learning. In *Proceedings of the Ninth National Conference on Artificial Intelligence*, Anaheim, California, 1991.

[54] Matthew T. Mason, Alan D. Christiansen, and Tom M. Mitchell. Experiments in robot learning. In *Proceedings of the Sixth International Workshop on Machine Learning*, pages 141–145, Ithaca, New York, 1989. Morgan Kaufmann.

[55] John McCarthy and Patrick J. Hayes. Some philosophical problems from the standpoint of artificial intelligence. In B. Meltzer and D. Michie, editors, *Machine Intelligence 4*. Edinburgh University Press, Edinburgh, 1969.

[56] Bartlett W. Mel. Building and using mental models in a sensory-motor domain: A connectionist approach. In *Proceedings of the Fifth International Conference on Machine Learning*, pages 207–213, Ann Arbor, Michigan, 1988.

[57] Ryszard S. Michalski. A theory and methodology of inductive learning. In Ryszard S. Michalski, Jaime G. Carbonell, and Tom M. Mitchell, editors, *Machine Learning: An Artificial Intelligence Approach*, chapter 4. Tioga, 1983.

[58]   D. Michie and R. A. Chambers. boxes: An experiment in adaptive control. In E. Dale and D. Michie, editors, *Machine Intelligence 2*. Oliver and Boyd, Edinburgh, 1968.

[59]   Donald Michie. Machine learning in the next five years. In *Proceedings of the Third European Working Session on Learning*, pages 107–122, Glasgow, 1988.

[60]   W. Thomas Miller III. Sensor-based control of robotic manipulators using a general learning algorithm. *IEEE Journal of Robotics and Automation*, RA-3(2):157–165, 1987.

[61]   Marvin L. Minsky. *Theory of Neural-Analog Reinforcement Systems and Its Application to the Brain-Model Problem*. PhD thesis, Princeton University, Princeton, New Jersey, 1954.

[62]   Marvin L. Minsky and Seymour Papert. *Perceptrons: An Introduction to Computational Geometry*. The MIT Press, Cambridge, Massachusetts, 1969.

[63]   Tom M. Mitchell. Version spaces: A candidate elimination approach to rule learning. In *Proceedings of the International Joint Conference on Artificial Intelligence*, pages 305–310, Cambridge, Massachusetts, 1977.

[64]   Tom M. Mitchell. Generalization as search. *Artificial Intelligence*, 18(2):203–226, 1982.

[65]   Tom M. Mitchell. The need for biases in learning generalizations. In Jude W. Shavlik and Thomas G. Dietterich, editors, *Readings in Machine Learning*. Morgan Kaufmann, San Mateo, California, 1990.

[66]   Andrew W. Moore. Acquisition of dynamic control knowledge for a robotic manipulator. In *Proceedings of the Seventh International Conference on Machine Learning*, pages 244–252, Austin, Texas, 1990. Morgan Kaufmann.

[67]   Edward F. Moore. Gedanken experiments on sequential machines. In *Automata Studies*, pages 129–153. Princeton University Press, Princeton, New Jersey, 1956.

[68]   Paul Munro. A dual back-propagation scheme for scalar reward learning. In *Proceedings of the Ninth Conference of the Cognitive Science Society*, pages 165–176, Seattle, Washington, 1987.

[69]   Kumpati Narendra and M. A. L. Thathachar. *Learning Automata: An Introduction*. Prentice-Hall, Englewood Cliffs, New Jersey, 1989.

[70]   Ulrich Nehmzow, Tim Smithers, and John Hallam. Steps towards intelligent robots. Technical Report 502, Department of Artificial Intelligence, University of Edinburgh, Edinburgh, Scotland, 1990.

[71]   Nils J. Nilsson. *Learning Machines*. McGraw-Hill, New York, 1965. Second edition, Morgan Kaufmann, 1990.

[72]   J. Ross Quinlan. Learning efficient classification procedures and their application to chess end games. In Ryszard S. Michalski, Jaime G. Carbonell, and Tom M. Mitchell, editors, *Machine Learning: An Artificial Intelligence Approach*, chapter 15. Tioga, 1983.

172   References

[73] Ronald L. Rivest and Robert E. Schapire. A new approach to unsupervised learning in deterministic environments. In *Proceedings of the Fourth International Workshop on Machine Learning*, pages 364–375, Irvine, California, 1987. Morgan Kaufmann.

[74] Sheldon M. Ross. *Introduction to Stochastic Dynamic Programming*. Academic Press, New York, 1983.

[75] D. E. Rumelhart, G. E. Hinton, and R. J. Williams. Learning internal representations by error propagation. In David E. Rumelhart and James L. McClelland, editors, *Parallel Distributed Processing*, volume 1, chapter 8. The MIT Press, Cambridge, Massachusetts, 1986.

[76] Stuart J. Russell. *The Use of Knowledge in Analogy and Induction*. Pitman Publishing, London, 1989.

[77] A. L. Samuel. Some studies in machine learning using the game of checkers. *IBM Journal of Research and Development*, 3:211–229, 1959. Reprinted in E. A. Feigenbaum and J. Feldman, editors, *Computers and Thought*, McGraw-Hill, New York 1963.

[78] A. L. Samuel. Some studies in machine learning using the game of checkers. II—Recent progress. *IBM Journal of Research and Development*, pages 601–617, 1967.

[79] Jeffrey C. Schlimmer. *Concept Acquisition Through Representational Adjustment*. PhD thesis, University of California, Irvine, Irvine, California, 1987.

[80] Jeffrey C. Schlimmer. Incremental adjustment of representations for learning. In *Proceedings of the Fourth International Workshop on Machine Learning*, pages 79–90, Ann Arbor, Michigan, 1987.

[81] Jeffrey C. Schlimmer. Learning and representation change. In *Proceedings of the Sixth National Conference on Artificial Intelligence*, volume 2, pages 511–515, Seattle, Washington, 1987. Morgan Kaufmann.

[82] Jeffrey C. Schlimmer and Richard H. Granger, Jr. Beyond incremental processing: Tracking concept drift. In *Proceedings of the Fifth National Conference on Artificial Intelligence*, volume 1, pages 502–507, Philadelphia, Pennsylvania, 1986. Morgan Kaufmann.

[83] Jeffrey C. Schlimmer and Richard H. Granger, Jr. Incremental learning from noisy data. *Machine Learning*, 1(3):317–354, 1986.

[84] Oliver G. Selfridge and Richard S. Sutton. Training and tracking in robotics. In *Proceedings of the Ninth International Joint Conference on Artificial Intelligence*, pages 670–672, Los Angeles, California, 1985. Morgan Kaufmann.

[85] Wei-Min Shen. *Learning from the Environment Based on Percepts and Actions*. PhD thesis, Carnegie Mellon University, Pittsburgh, Pennsylvania, 1989.

[86] Herbert A. Simon. *The Sciences of the Artificial*. The MIT Press, Cambridge, Massachusetts, second edition, 1982.

[87] Satinder Pal Singh. Transfer of learning by composing solutions of elemental sequential tasks. *Machine Learning*, 8(3):323–340, 1992.

[88] George W. Snedecor and William G. Cochran. *Statistical Methods*. Iowa State University Press, Ames, Iowa, eighth edition, 1989.

[89] Richard S. Sutton. *Temporal Credit Assignment in Reinforcement Learning*. PhD thesis, University of Massachusetts, Amherst, Massachusetts, 1984.

[90] Richard S. Sutton. Learning to predict by the method of temporal differences. *Machine Learning*, 3(1):9–44, 1988.

[91] Richard S. Sutton. Integrated architectures for learning, planning, and reacting based on approximating dynamic programming. In *Proceedings of the Seventh International Conference on Machine Learning*, Austin, Texas, 1990. Morgan Kaufmann.

[92] Richard S. Sutton and Brian Pinette. The learning of world models by connectionist networks. In *Proceedings of the Seventh Annual Conference of the Cognitive Science Society*, pages 54–64, 1985.

[93] M. A. L. Thathachar and P. S. Sastry. A new approach to the design of reinforcement schemes for learning automata. *IEEE Transactions on Systems, Man, and Cybernetics*, SMC-15(1):168–175, 1985.

[94] M. L. Tsetlin. *Automaton Theory and Modeling of Biological Systems*. Academic Press, New York, New York, 1973.

[95] L. G. Valiant. A theory of the learnable. *Communications of the ACM*, 27(11):1134–1142, 1984.

[96] L. G. Valiant. Learning disjunctions of conjunctions. In *Proceedings of the International Joint Conference on Artificial Intelligence*, volume 1, pages 560–566, Los Angeles, California, 1985. Morgan Kaufmann.

[97] C. J. C. H. Watkins. *Learning from Delayed Rewards*. PhD thesis, King's College, Cambridge, 1989.

[98] C. J. C. H. Watkins and P. Dayan. Q-learning. *Machine Learning*, 8(3):279–292, 1992.

[99] Paul J. Werbos. Generalization of backpropagation with application to a recurrent gas market model. *Neural Networks*, 1:339–356, 1988.

[100] Steven D. Whitehead. Complexity and cooperation in q-learning. In *Proceedings of the Eighth International Workshop on Machine Learning*, Evanston, Illinois, 1991. Morgan Kaufmann.

[101] Steven D. Whitehead and Dana H. Ballard. A role for anticipation in reactive systems that learn. In *Proceedings of the Sixth International Workshop on Machine Learning*, pages 354–357, Ithaca, New York, 1989. Morgan Kaufmann.

[102] Steven D. Whitehead and Dana H. Ballard. Learning to perceive and act by trial and error. *Machine Learning*, 7(1):45–83, 1991.

[103] B. Widrow and S. D. Stearns. *Adaptive Signal Processing*. Prentice Hall, Englewood Cliffs, New Jersey, 1985.

[104] Bernard Widrow, Narendra K. Gupta, and Sidhartha Maitra. Punish/reward: Learning with a critic in adaptive threshold systems. *IEEE Transactions on Systems, Man, and Cybernetics*, SMC-3(5):455–465, 1973.

[105] Bernard Widrow and Marcian E. Hoff. Adaptive switching circuits. In *IRE WESCON Convention Record*, New York, New York, 1960. Reprinted in *Neurocomputing: Foundations of Research*, James A. Anderson and Edward Rosenfeld, editors, The MIT Press, Cambridge, Massachusetts, 1988.

[106] Ronald J. Williams. Reinforcement learning in connectionist networks: A mathematical analysis. Technical Report ICS-8605, Institute for Cognitive Science, University of California, San Diego, La Jolla, California, 1986.

[107] Ronald J. Williams. A class of gradient-estimating algorithms for reinforcement learning in neural networks. In *Proceedings of the IEEE First International Conference on Neural Networks*, San Diego, California, 1987.

[108] Ronald J. Williams. On the use of backpropagation in associative reinforcement learning. In *Proceedings of the IEEE International Conference on Neural Networks*, San Diego, California, 1988.

[109] Ian H. Witten. An adaptive optimal controller for discrete-time markov environments. *Information and Control*, 34:286–295, 1977.

Index